PUB WALKS IN WILT

90 POLYGON
FROM 36 WILTSHIRE AND

CHARLES WESTAWAY

First Edition

Greensward Publications

FRONT COVER: The Spread Eagle Inn, Stourton

Frontispiece: Bristol High Cross, Stourton

ACKNOWLEDGEMENTS

Mere thanks seem inadequate for the total contribution made by Mrs Christine Stevenson to this book. Chris not only had much to do with its conception, she accompanied me on many walks, often waiting patiently in a cold car while I checked some detail away up a hill. The speed and accuracy of her typing have been first rate and her patience continued throughout the changes arising from my third and fourth thoughts in the drafting into proof reading. Yet above all has been her unflagging encouragement.

Thanks too must go to the many helpful owners, tenants and landlords for much of the information on which this book relies. Also to numerous landowners, farmers (especially The Earl of Cardigan of Savernake Forest, Mr Cubbon of Bowood Estates, and Mr Bryant of Stowford) and farm workers who have without exception been pleasant as well as helpful.

Thanks also to publishers William Heinemann Ltd for kind permission to include the quotation from J. B. Priestly's *English Journey*; to Mrs Myfanwy Thomas and publishers Faber and Faber for allowing me to reprint Edward Thomas' poem *The Combe* in full; and to the Andrew Young estate for allowing me to use his poem *Wiltshire Downs* in full.

PUBLISHERS NOTE
While all reasonable care has been taken regarding the accuracy of the information contained in this publication, neither the author, nor the publisher, nor the printer can accept liability for any inaccuracies. Land use changes, pubs and inns change hands, opening times (especially with summer extensions) may change, menus are often daily matters. Authorial slips have been known, printing errors may occur.

All comments are very welcome and it is often as a result of public response that future improvements may be made. So, having used the book, do please write to the publisher at the address below.

Published by: *Greensward Publications, 116 Wessex Oval, Wareham, Dorset BH20 4BS*
Typeset by: *Amberwood Graphics, 257 High Street, Swanage, Dorset BH19 2NG*
Printed by: *The Friary Press, Bridport Road, Dorchester, Dorset DT1 1JL*

ISBN 1 872888 00 3

THE COMBE

The combe was ever dark, ancient and dark.
Its mouth is stopped with bramble, thorn and briar;
And no one scrambles over the sliding chalk
By beech and yew and perishing juniper
Down the half precipices of its sides, with roots
And rabbit holes for steps. The sun of Winter,
The moon of Summer, and all the singing birds
Except the missel-thrush that loves juniper,
Are quite shut out. But far more ancient and dark
The combe looks since they killed the badger there,
Dug him out and gave him to the hounds,
That most ancient Briton of English beasts.

Edward Thomas

WILTSHIRE DOWNS

The cuckoo's double note
Loosened like bubbles from a drowning throat
Floats through the air
In mockery of pipit, lark and stare.

The stable-boys thud by
Their horses slinging divots at the sky
And with bright hooves
Printing the sodden turf with lucky grooves.

As still as a windhover
A shepherd in his flapping coat leans over
His tall sheep-crook
And shearlings, tegs and yoes cons like a book.

And one tree-crowned long barrow
Stretched like a sow that has brought forth her farrow
Hides a king's bones
Lying like broken sticks among the stones.

Andrew Young

INTRODUCTION

I enjoy walking the countryside. Often I am happy to walk two to four miles, yet at times I prefer a greater distance. At the end of a walk I find myself in need of refreshment. What better than to use a pub or inn as a base? The aim of this guide is to provide a number of walks of different distances from pubs and inns offering some interest and hospitality. The criteria are purely personal.

> *Clamping the past on to the present, turning history and art into exact topography, makes no appeal to me; I do not care where the battle was fought or the queen slept, nor out of what window the poet looked; but a landscape rich in these vague associations - some of them without a name - gives me deep pleasure......*

J. B. Priestly *English Journey*

While I am inclined to share this attitude to landscape, I recognise that many of my readers may feel the need of some background information, though I cannot but fail to satisfy all tastes. This is not a text book, neither is it an historical nor nature guide. It is intended as a practical guide for the walker who likes a safe and comfortable base. People carry with them their own knowledge and expertise. If, like myself, walkers prefer to do their own research into whatever takes their fancies rather than rely upon the definitive guide or acknowledged expert (a happy condition in which I cannot claim to find myself), this book allows them that freedom. See a church, a barrow, a monument to take your interest, investigate it now and research it later as thoroughly as you will or, having savoured it a moment, pass on by. Yet I feel some context ought to be provided. I have, therefore, chosen to 'sprinkle'. All the walks are briefly introduced, sometimes with a little history, sometimes with a little geology, sometimes with a little anecdote. The descriptions of the pubs and inns contain somewhat more historical and architectural information, because customers tend to have an interest in something they are actively using and it can provide a subject of conversation at the bar. Similarly, if you are travelling to an unfamiliar location, it can be reassuring to feel you know something of your hosts and that there is at least the possibility of a warm welcome. Many years ago I walked into a pub in North Wales. All conversation immediately stopped and all heads turned to stare. I was the stranger. Having placed my order at the bar, conversation resumed - in Welsh. While I enjoy the dynamics of historical commentary, when in the countryside give me not the dusty historical fact but the anecdote redolent of life and the living countryside itself.

For all pubs and inns I have given a map reference number from the Ordnance Survey 'Landranger' series. Where walks continue on to other maps I have indicated these in brackets. The grid reference number refers to the site of the pub or inn. Instructions for using these are included on all O.S. maps.

I have tried to take into account that some walkers are vegetarians, children or dogs. While these remain minority groups, nevertheless I have tried to avoid the impression that they are less important — they are not — by sometimes placing their catering needs earlier in the text than those of meat-eating adults. Dogs will just have to accept that they do happen to be placed last.

Unfortunately, not all publicans have been able to confirm information by the time of going to press, so in some cases opening times and other details are unavailable.

Of the language and abbreviations used to describe the walks a few words should be said. As a practical guide, a series of instructions, it seemed to me the text required clarity rather than style. To this end I have attempted to employ three devices:

a) a system of abbreviations as set out below
b) a deliberately repetitive style
c) sentences of reasonable length

Rather than repeat simple words and phrases, like 'turn left' and 'bear right', it seemed possible to reduce them to a set of abbreviations. However, abbreviations apply to movement rather than position. For example, an instruction to move towards the left hand hedge is represented as 'Make way to the **LH** hedge', whereas an indication of the position of a hedge relative to whatever movement the instruction involves is represented as 'Keeping close to the hedge on the left, go on...' and is not abbreviated. By using a repetitive style with precision of language, I hope the reader becomes so familiar with the style that the meaning and intention are immediately apprehended. Any written instructions should tend towards short sentences. The aim, and my hope, is that the reader may swiftly establish meaning by way of quick glances rather than long study. Please let me have your comments.

Unfortunately, I have not been able to include all the routes I would have liked. Although a route to Stonehenge has been included, the absence of suitable hostelries in the vicinity has forced a degree of repetition I would have wished to avoid. Fyfield Down, west of Marlborough, with its Celtic field systems and barrows is absent — I could find no pub of sufficient interest that was within a realistic distance. A different problem exists in north-east Wiltshire near Swindon. It was extremely difficult to match the requirements of a basically circular route of interest with a pub of interest. Similarly on the Salisbury Plains, with the additional problem of limited access due to military control — there is a large hole in the county map on page 10. Pressure from other locations in the region determined the final choice. I would be glad for any information towards solving these problems for any future editions.

Do wear sensible clothing. Experienced walkers know how to cope with wind and rain. For those starting out, a few tips may be helpful. To stay warm insulate your body heat with layers of light clothing — heavy sweaters are fine for standing around, not for walking. To stay dry wear waterproofs. Footwear can be a problem. A farmer complained to me that young ladies would knock on the farmhouse door to ask if there were an alternative route around the farmyard as they didn't want to spoil their shoes — at the time we were standing up to our ankles in an unspeakable mess, but that is what farmyards are like. Wellies, preferably, or boots in winter; strong shoes in summer, but even then expect to get them wet.

For many the attraction of walking in Wiltshire and Avon lies in their variety. Partly, this variety is due to the geology and the resulting topography. I have always felt it useful in the countryside to have some awareness of geography and geology. Hopefully, what follows will be of use to some — if not all.

Chalk downland covers the south and east of the region almost entirely. There are two exceptions. In the south-eastern corner Wiltshire encroaches upon the sandy heathland of The New Forest. To the west, between Warminster and Frome, the heavy soil of the clay vale sweeps north-eastward towards Swindon. Yet the downs are not uniform. They are scored by a number of valleys. Chief amongst these is the Avon valley where the river flows south to Salisbury. There are also the west-east Vale of Wardour between Semley and Wilton, the Wylye valley between Warminster and Salisbury, and the Vale of Pewsey — striking not only for its northern flank of steep-sided hills, but for its lack of a natural watercourse. Between these valleys stretch the Salisbury Plains. With the erosion of the chalk in these valleys, other rocks appear on the surface to give further variety within the overall distribution of chalk. Nor are the chalk hills themselves similar. The angle of tilt of the beds where they reach the surface determines their appearance. In the Vale of Pewsey, where the angle is shallow, the hills rise to over 900 feet and are steep-sided. Yet at Savernake Forest the forty-five degree tilt shows only a narrow and unimpressive escarpment. The characteristic appearance of the downs is of rolling hills covered, when not ploughed, with short grass surrounding a copse of beeches on top and, occasionally, crossed by creamy tracks sprinkled with flints. However, where deposits of clay and flints top the hills, the beeches may give way to oaks. Also the onward march of the quick-turnover conifer plantation is increasingly evident, and it can double as a game nursery for the shooting syndicates. The presence of the various White Horses indicates the thinness of the soil. This makes it fine sheep country, historically linked with the wool trade, and drovers' tracks are frequent. Buildings are more likely to be of brick and slate, sometimes using local flint and thatch. The longevity of human settlement in this area is well known. Before the Saxon invasion the uplands, as at Fyfield Down and Barbury Castle, were preferred to the densely wooded valleys. The total population was not great and was widely distributed. The Roman occupation marked the landscape with a substantial road system which today remains in many forms from major trunk roads to more peaceful tracks, some of which appear in this collection: The Clarendon Way, and drovers' tracks where original Roman roads were subsequently utilised for the movement of livestock and upon which, often at remote points, inns were established to service the traffic — The Shears at Cadley is an example. In the sheltered valleys you may notice hedgerow plantlife, like primrose and violet or the climbing bryony and traveller's joy. On the downs the open grassland may be home to scabious, wild thyme and salad burnet, while at the appropriate season skylark, yellowhammer and corn-bunting may be seen. There are many fields on these walks from which you may pick, if confident of identifying them accurately, wild mushrooms. The summer of '89 produced an abundance for the kitchen at home. Unfortunately, I am under strict instructions not to identify precise locations.

As only one walk — Seend Cleeve — in this collection lies in the clay vale, I have little to say other than one's boots can become infuriatingly muddy.

A different landscape entirely is produced in the north-west of the region by the Cotswold limestone belt, again with its own internal variations. There is the deeply cut Avon valley. There are similar narrow, steep-sided and wooded valleys, like By Brook between Castle Combe and Ford. (So deep is this valley that the Fosse Way was kept to the west, turning only after it had passed the valley head). Alternatively, there is the flat upland dip-slope south-east to the clay vale. The countryside around Sherston is typical and Easton Grey is well named. J. B. Priestly has described Cotswold limestone as warm, weathering to browns and yellows, yet here the grey-green of the buildings is dominant. The hedgerows of the chalklands and clay lowlands are less evident, the characteristic dry-stone walls resulting from the availability of stone.

Finally,

PLEASE REMEMBER THE COUNTRY CODE

- enjoy and respect the countryside
- guard against all risk of fire
- fasten all gates
- keep dogs under control
- do not cause damage to property
- do not drop litter
- do not pick wild flowers nor dig up plants
- do not stray from public paths across farmland

and have a good time.

Charles Westaway

KEY TO ABBREVIATIONS IN THE TEXT

X	cross	**L**	left
TL	turn left	**R**	right
TR	turn right	**LH**	left hand
BL	bear left	**RH**	right hand
BR	bear right	**ULH**	upper left hand
CL	curve left	**URH**	upper right hand
CR	curve right	**LLH**	lower left hand
FL	fork left	**LRH**	lower right hand
FR	fork right		

KEY TO SKETCH MAPS

narrow or undefined path (with very steep ascent)
grass or gravel track (with steep ascent)
metalled road, lane or drive
stile or fence
small gate
large gate
wire gate
gap in hedge or fence
bridge
arch
posts
building
church
monument, column or obelisk
triangulation point
lake or pond
stream, river or canal
river with weir
canal with lock
railway line
trees
car park and/or picnic area

WALK NUMBERS AND THEIR LOCATIONS

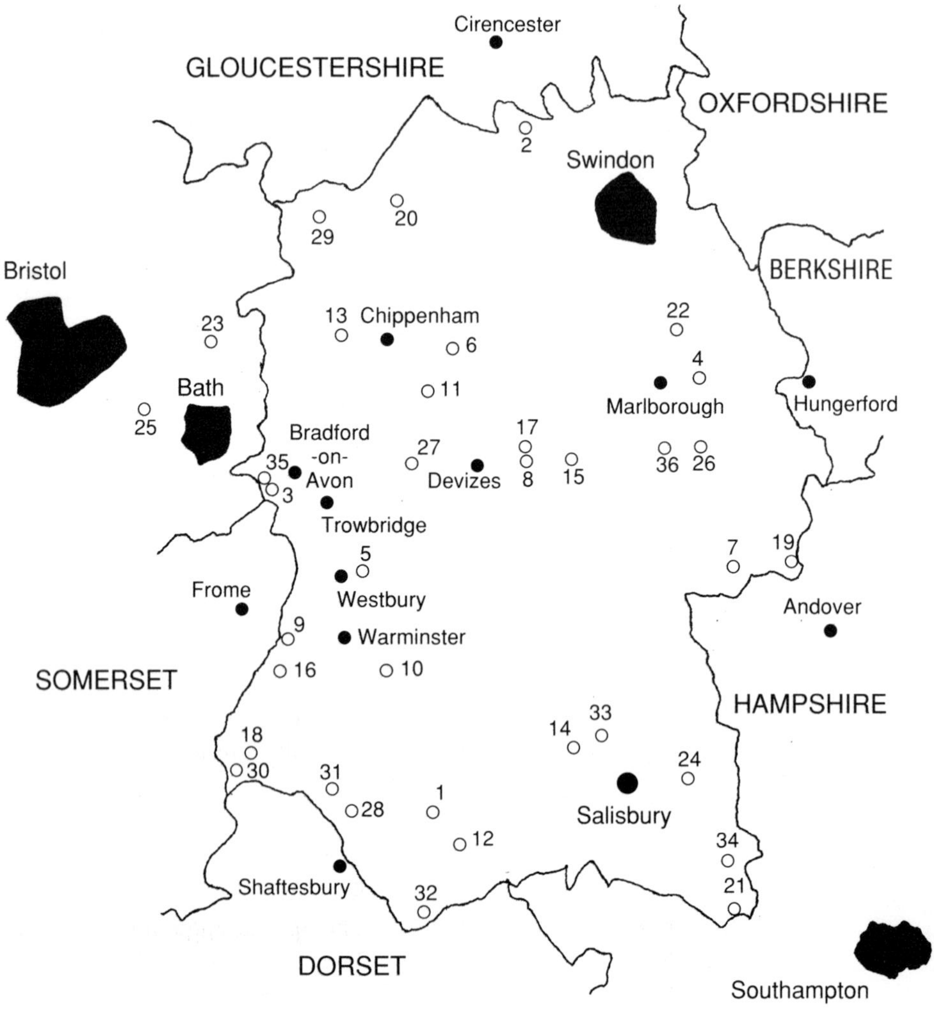

CONTENTS

O.S. MAP NO. 184 : 956 265

Turn left off the A30 about seven miles north-east of Shaftesbury.
Turn right off the A30 about ten miles south-west of Wilton.
Parking is available at the rear of the pub, including a large paddock area, and out front.

HOURS:	Sunday	12.00 - 3.00	:	CLOSED
	Weekdays	11.00 - 2.30	:	6.30 - 11.00
	Saturday	11.00 - 2.30	:	6.30 - 11.00

N.B. Closed Sunday evening and all day Monday.

This stone building, with flint and brick fascia, was built about 1825 as an ale and beer house for workers on the Wardour estate. Today it has one very comfortable bar with a dining area, and a small restaurant. Mr and Mrs Hamshere put considerable emphasis on the serving of food and The Maypole Inn is closer to being a restaurant than a village pub. A substantial snack menu has a welcome variety of ploughman's and sandwiches freshly prepared with a choice of bread which includes wholemeal. The main menu also exhibits some variety. From a choice of nine starters it is possible to move to a main course like breaded breast of chicken with a crab and pink peppercorn filling or breaded turkey with asparagus and ham filling (all ham is home-cooked). Six different fish dishes are available. Desserts too are plentiful, and only real dairy ice-cream is used. Vegetarian meals are separately available, though children's meals are not. The bar serves Butcombe Bitter, Wadworth's 6X and Ringwood Fortyniner.

No children under five years of age are allowed on the premises, although between five and fourteen they may sit in the dining area.
Dogs are not allowed.

The Vale of Wardour lies between chalk downland to north and south, and is the result of the erosion of this chalk, chiefly by the River Nadder. This action has revealed a geological variety of clays, sands and limestones which have created an area of considerable beauty. These walks take in the ruined castle and estate which give the valley its name, lakes, woodland and conifer plantations.

ANSTY — THE MAYPOLE INN

Walk 1	**3 miles**	**Parts A B G**
Walk 2	**5 miles**	**Parts A C D F G**
Walk 3	**5½ miles**	**Parts A C E F G**

A From the inn **TL** up the lane to the junction with another lane from the right. Here **TR** through a metal gate into a field. **X** the field to a stile on the far side. **X** the next field to the far hedge and **TR** to a metal gate. **TL** into the next field and slightly **BR** to a black metal double gate. **TL** up the lane and immediately **R** through a metal gate into a field. Slightly **BR** to a stile opposite. **BR** through a spinney to exit at a thatched stone cottage by the entrance to *Squalls Estate.* **X** the stile to the right of the driveway. Go directly uphill, passing through a broad gap in a wire fence between two woods. Keeping close to the fence on the left, continue to a stile at the end. **TL** over the stile into a wood. **BL** down a path at about 45° for some 300 yards to exit over a stile into a field. **TL** through a metal gate into the next field. **TR** and keeping close to the wire fence, pass through a metal gate into the adjoining field. **BL** over the crest of a rise and pass through a wooden gate into a lane. **TL** along the lane, past *Highwood Lodge,* to the driveway of *Old Wardour Castle.* **TL** to the ruins.

B At the car park, with the ruins to the right, go straight up the path climbing behind the ruins into the wood. Pass under an old stone bridge and continue up and out of the wood onto a broad grass track between two fields. Continue along this track until it is crossed by another broad track. Just beyond is another junction, at which **TR**.

C Continue along the track between the ruins and the lake to a stone arch.

D **FL** under the arch into the wood. Shortly **FR**, continuing along the main track.

E **FR** down the **RH** edge of a field, pass a lake and **X** a stile by a wooden gate. Continue uphill to pass through another gate into a wood. **TL** along a broad track and follow it round to join another track, at which **TR**.

F By a bungalow exit onto a driveway. **TL** along the drive to a farm. **BR** through the farm and **TR** in the centre along a track straight ahead. Follow the track between two fields and **CL** to a junction. **TR** and immediately **TR** again on a parallel track.

G Shortly pass into a lane. Continue past *Combe House* to **TL** through the second metal gate. **BR** past a telegraph pole towards a metal gate in a wire fence on the far side. Go through and **X** the field. Directly opposite are 2 metal gates. Take the **LH** gate directly towards a line of trees ahead. Go down the slightly overgrown path between the trees as it drops below the fields either side. **X** the stile ahead, and **CR** to exit opposite the first gate of the walk. **TR** to the inn.

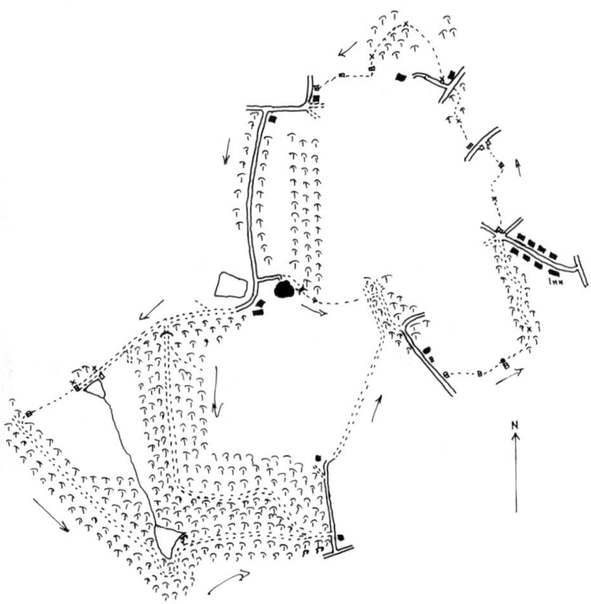

O.S. MAP NO. 173 (also 163) : 043 938

From the B4040, turn left about two miles east of Minety or turn right about one mile west of Cricklade. The inn is located in Gosditch.
There are two large car parks, and it is possible to park along the roadside in Gosditch.

HOURS:	Sunday	12.00 - 3.00	:	7.00 - 10.30
	Weekdays	11.30 - 2.30	:	6.00 - 11.00
	Saturday	11.30 - 2.30	:	6.00 - 11.00

Of Cotswold stone and slate this building is reputed to date from the sixteenth century. Hosts Michael and Frances Nevin informed me that it had originally been two separate cottages; first one became an inn, then the other. There are two bars and a family room. The lounge has original beams, apparently, and is attractively furnished with a miscellany of round-back, ladderback and simple boxwood chairs. A gravy-boat collection hangs from the ceiling and is complemented by a wide range of memorabilia — spinning-wheel, wind-up gramophone, miniature glockenspiel. Set in an alcove behind a wrought iron gate is an early collection of Dickens and The Encyclopædia Brittanica. All this is imaginatively lit by the soft glow of candlelight.

Being a Courage house, Best and Directors are served. The usual variety of snacks is available, while the main menu offers, for example, home-made soup or deep-fried garlic mushrooms, followed by sirloin with pepper, brandy and cream sauce, concluding with home-made apple pie or hot chocolate fudge cake. A single vegetarian dish is always available — a vegetarian pie when I was there.

There is a large garden with putting green, swings and play frame.

Children may, of course, come into the family room.
Dogs are not allowed inside.

ASHTON KEYNES — THE HORSE AND JOCKEY INN

Not 'chocolate box' but 'lived in', this pretty village of subtly-shaded Cotswold limestone nevertheless lies, like Malmesbury, on the edge where the stone dips under damper clays and the presence of water gives rise to more settlement. Here, then, in a water park, are two walks around previous gravel pits now given over to wild life or water-sports enthusiasts, current areas of extraction, and briefly along the banks of the gentle upper Thames. Flat and easy. Diversions may be in operation here; follow instructions and signs. Swimming is prohibited in all but the designated areas. For further information phone **0285 861459**

Walk 1	**3 miles**	**Part A**
Walk 2	**7 miles**	**Part B**

A **TL** to a T-junction and **TR** along a road. Soon **TL** through a small gate and along a footpath. Shortly **TL** along the Thames, **X** a bridge and on to **X** a footbridge just beyond and at 45° to a vehicle bridge. Immediately **X** a stile onto a path and follow it to **TL** at a junction ahead. Soon **X** another stile, then **CR** along the path which goes along an embankment up to a distant stile and out onto a road. Carefully **X** the road and stile opposite. **TR** along the path parallel to the road to reach a cottage by a drive signed *Cotswold Community*. Carefully again **X** the road and the stile by double metal gates opposite. Follow this track for some distance as it meanders round to pass a manor house and shortly **X** a stile by the entrance gates. **TR** along the road, over the Thames, and **TL** into *Gosditch* and the inn.

B **TR** to the end of the road. **TL** along the main village street, then **TR** along *Back Street*. At the end **CR** and immediately **TL** along a broad drive to shortly **FR** along a bridle path. Follow this path to a road and **TL**. About ¼ mile along **TR** over a stile by a metal gate into a field and **X** diagonally to go over another stile and footbridge along a path round a lake and over a third stile onto a lane. **TR** and, just around the curve, **TL** over a stile by a gate. Keeping close to the hedge on the left, go on to **X** a stile by a gate, then **TR** along a right hand hedge round to **X** a bridge onto a broad grassy path. *(This is the course of an old railway and you are now in Gloucestershire).* **TL** and follow it straight ahead, across a road, through a car park and on to another road. **TL** along this road, through the village of *South Cerney* to **TL** just after the village cross along *Broadway Lane.* Go straight on and **TR** along a narrow path beside the last houses. Go on over a bridge and **TL** through a gap in a hedge into a field. **TL** again back along the hedge to **TR** at the end of the field and follow the meandering path to a stile and over on to a road. Carefully **X** the road and follow a path along the left hand side of a car-park/picnic area. This leads by new diggings, along a zig-zag path, and beside cottages out to *Back Street.* Retrace steps to the inn.

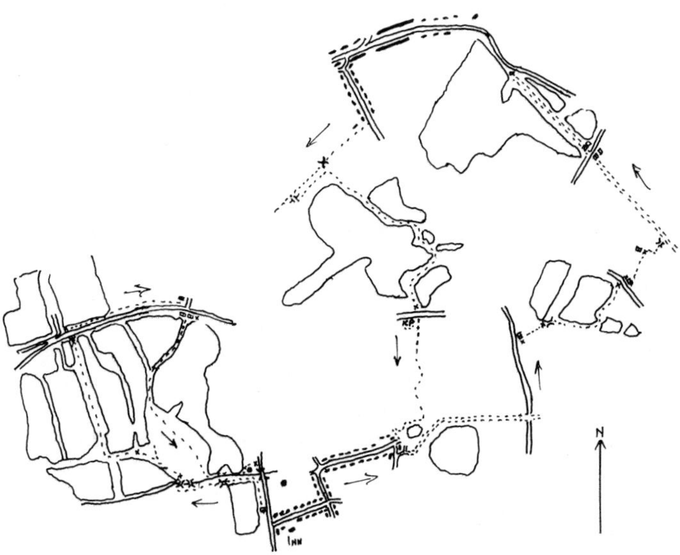

Avon Valley from Avoncliffe aqueduct

O.S. MAP NO. 173 (also 172) : 805 599

From Bradford-on-Avon, take the B3109 south to the outskirts where it sharply crosses the river. Here turn right towards Avoncliffe. Just before entering the village, take the first right down a narrow lane to the aqueduct. (About two miles from Bradford centre).

Alternatively, take the minor road from Bradford-on-Avon to Avoncliffe railway station and walk across the aqueduct. (About one and a half miles from Bradford centre).

The inn has no car park of its own and, consequently, parking is severely limited. The best possibilities are at the end of the approach lane south of the aqueduct or the half dozen bays above the station on the north side.

HOURS:	Sunday	12.00 - 3.00	:	7.00 - 10.30
	Weekdays	11.00 - 3.00	:	6.30 - 11.00
	Saturday	11.00 - 3.00	:	6.30 - 11.00

This has to be one of the most picturesque settings for any of the houses in this publication. The inn stands low in the Avon valley overlooking the river below, the Kennet and Avon canal behind and the aqueduct at the same level to one side. Terraced seating drops down towards the river. Walk the few yards to the aqueduct and gaze up and down the length of the river and steeply-wooded banks.

The building is of painted limestone with a limestone-walled interior and a putative sixteenth century fireplace. A single bar is divided into two areas. David and Gwen Sawyer, the new hosts, are planning refurbishment, although it was already very comfortable when I saw it. They serve Usher's Best, Ruddle's Best and County, Smiles' Best, and Tanglefoot by Hall and Woodhouse. Gwen assures me that all food is home-made and freshly cooked and it seems this is to be a speciality. Snacks include home-made steak pies. Starters of butterfly prawns with garlic dip or mushrooms with blue cheese and garlic dip may be followed by a poached salmon steak (fresh up from Brixham, I'm told) or fresh crab. Desserts include seasonal fruit pies and crumbles. Vegetarians may be offered a lasagne, quiche or curry. Best of luck to the new owners.

Children are allowed on the premises.
Dogs are not.

It is generally very difficult to walk in the Frome and Avon valleys near Bath without either following flat stretches along the river or climbing steep banks — or both! (Try Winsley, page 92). Here, however, the long walk gains height slowly and steadily as it passes along the Avon and, by their confluence, up the Frome to turn at Stowford over to Westwood for the steep descent to Avoncliffe. History and architecture are represented by the Avoncliffe aqueduct carrying the Kennet and Avon canal across the river, the ruined castle at Farleigh Hungerford and the manors of Westwood and Iford, the latter possessing a fine Italianate terraced garden. In some contrast the short walk offers an easy stroll by the river to return along the canal.

Walk 1	**1 mile**	**Part A**
Walk 2	**3 miles**	**Parts B C**
Walk 3	**5½ miles**	**Parts B D**

A **TL** and **CL** beside the canal round behind the inn. Shortly **FL** along the river for ½ mile, then **CR** up to the canal towpath by a swingbridge and return. (Try an alternative. **X** the bridge, **TR** along the far canal bank, **X** a pair of stiles and footbridge and go through a gap in a hedge ahead. Slightly **BL** up to **X** a stile on the corner of the wood above and continue to a lane which returns to the aqueduct).

B Go under the aqueduct and straight along a track past houses. As the track turns left to a field continue ahead along a path to **X** a stile by a metal gate into a meadow. Follow the river bank to pass through a small metal gate into another meadow. *(The confluence is to the right).* **TL** along the treeline to a small wooden gate at a road junction. Go along the road ahead to **X** a stile by a metal gate into a field. Go ahead to **CL** down to the river. Continue along the bank, **X** a stile by a wooden gate and on through double wooden gates onto a road. **TR** to *Iford Manor.*

C Continue ahead up a steep lane to a road above. **TL**, then **TR** along a bridleway signed *Upper Westwood.* **TR** into the village lane and immediately **TL** along a short drive between 2 houses. **X** a stile by a wooden gate into a field, then drop down to **X** another stile in the **LRH** corner. Go down steps, **TL** onto a narrow path and **CR** to **X** a stone stile into another field. **BR** down to **X** a stile by a wooden gate onto a track, then shortly **TR** to the inn.

D **TR** across the bridge, pass a house to the right and **TL** through a small metal gate before a house on the left. Follow the path along the bank through a series of gates and stiles to *Farleigh Hungerford Castle (see map).* **TL** down the road to **TR** over a stile into a field beyond the second of 2 bridges. Follow the path through a wire gate, over a stile by a metal gate to **BL** through a gap in a wire fence to the road by Stowford Farm.

(Please note that this path from Farleigh to Stowford Farm is not a public right of way but has been made available by kind permission of the owner, Mr Bryant, and may be closed for one day each year, in which case continue along the main road).

TR, then carefully **X** the road to go through a pair of metal gates onto a track between farm buildings. Go ahead to **X** a stile by a metal gate, then **CL** through a gap in a wire fence and immediately **BR** through a similar gap. Now **BL** up to **X** a stile by a metal gate in the **URH** corner into the next field and make way to **X** a stile in the far hedge. Continue towards *Westwood* church to **X** a stone stile ahead and across the next field to **X** a stile between 2 wooden gates in a stone wall. Exit onto a lane by *Westwood Manor.* **TR** to a T-junction and go on to **X** a stile by a metal gate behind the inn opposite. Make way towards a distant wind pump. **X** a pair of stiles in the far hedge, then **BL** to **X** another stile in a hedge ahead and on to **X** a stone stile in the next hedge ahead. Exit onto a lane and **BR** through the metal gate opposite. *(Ahead is Bradford-upon-Avon).* **CL** down to **X** 4 stiles *(see map).* At the fourth enter a wood above the canal. Continue to a lane and on down to the inn.

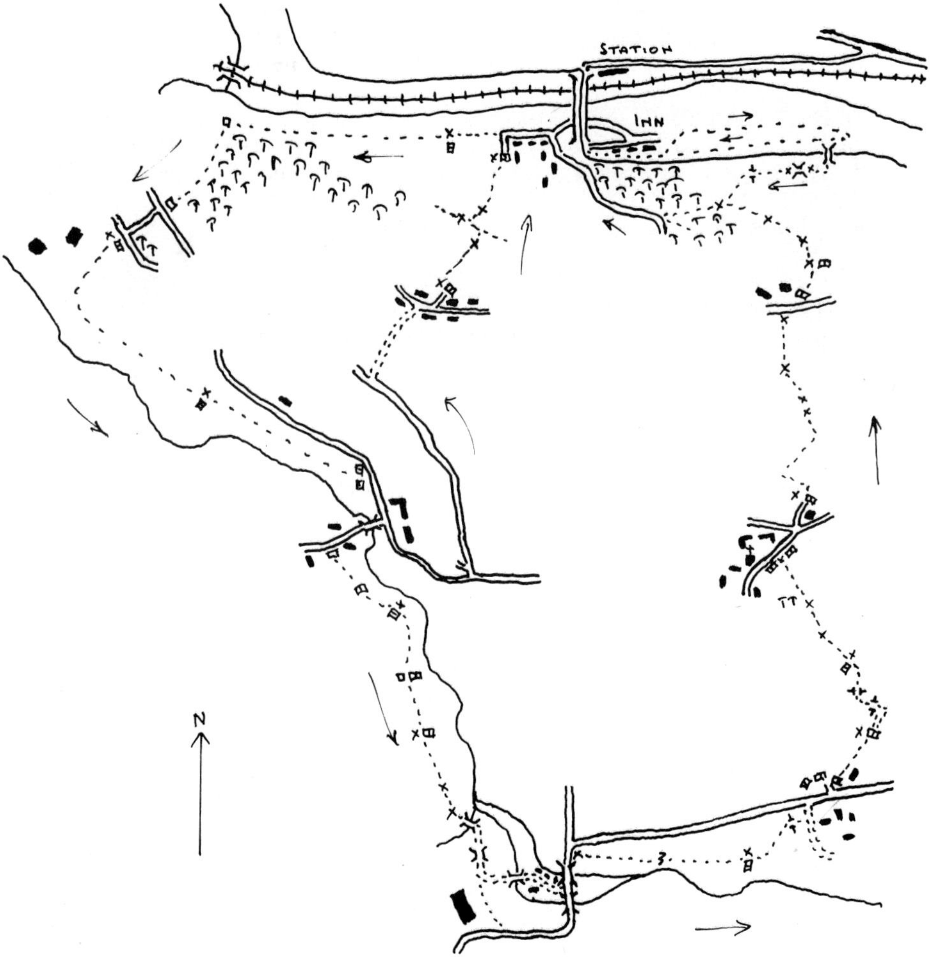
STATION
INN
N

O.S. MAP NO. 174 : 237 701

About three miles east of Marlborough on the road to Ramsbury.
There is an ample car park or park along the road.

HOURS:	Sunday	12.00 - 3.00	:	7.00 - 10.30
	Weekdays	11.00 - 3.00	:	6.00 - 11.00
	Saturday	11.00 - 3.00	:	6.00 - 11.00

Pleasantly located just above the River Kennet, there are two bars and a restaurant. Both lounge and restaurant have views over the river, as does the garden seating area.

The emphasis here is on food, especially fish and game. Start with scallops in madeira before moving to pheasant, duck or fillet of venison, or stay with fish to try lobster, mullet or sole. Vegetarians and children's meals are available separately. Draught ales are Wadworth's 6X, Archer's Best, and Marston's Pedigree.

Children are welcome.
Dogs in the public bar only.

A pleasant and straightforward stroll along the River Kennet and a wood above.

Walk 1	**3 miles**	**Parts A B**
Walk 2	**4½ miles**	**Parts A C**

A **TL** along the road. **TL** down a lane, over 2 bridges, and round a bend to a bridleway. **TL** over a stile and go up the grassy track, over another stile and past a farm. Continue to a metal gate, but **TR** to **X** a stile. **TL** along the edge of the field to directly enter the wood ahead. **BL** along a path to **X** 3 stiles in succession and onto a broad deeply-rutted track. **TL** along this track round to, and through, a large wooden gate. **TL** along another track, then **TR** to shortly **X** a junction and continue along a narrow path on the edge of the wood. Still in the wood, **TL** at the end of the field to the left, **X** a track, and ahead **TR** onto a broad track. **TL** and immediately **TR** at a junction. This soon becomes a leafy tunnel descending between fields.

B Continue to the bottom. **BL** past a house along a path to **X** 2 bridges and up to a road. **TL** to the pub.

C Soon **TR** and immediately **FL** through a small wooden gate. Go down to another small wooden gate and on to the bottom. **CL** over a bridge, **X** a stile by a metal gate, and **BL** towards a line of hawthorns left of the house ahead *(that this is a converted priory is still visible in the architecture).* **X** another bridge, go through a small wooden gate, and **TL** to go through the trees ahead, along the river bank and up to a stile into the spinney ahead. Go through to **X** another stile onto a road and **TL** to the pub.

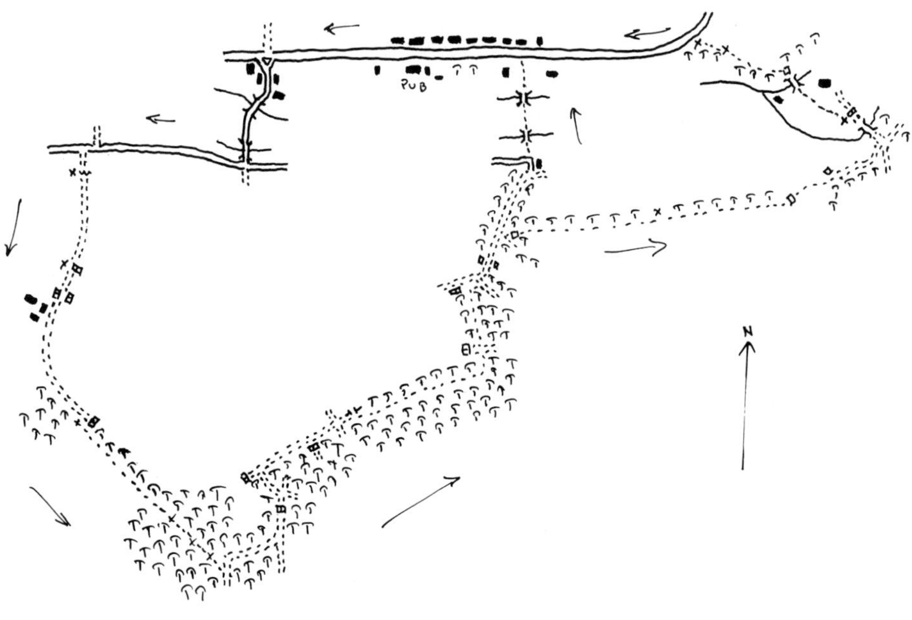

O.S. MAP NO. 184 : 914 525

In the centre of the village, on the B3098 about two miles east of Westbury.
Parking is plentiful in the forty-space car park and there are no restrictions on parking in the village.

HOURS:	Sunday	12.00 - 3.00	:	7.00 - 10.30
	Weekdays	11.30 - 2.30	:	6.00 - 11.00
	Saturday	11.30 - 2.30	:	6.00 - 11.00

Michael Considine, your host, informs me that this brick and red tile building dates from the eighteenth century when it was a terrace of three cottages. There are two bars and, what Michael describes as, 'a country-cottage style restaurant'. This serves a starter of butterfly prawns in orange juice and soy sauce or a roulade of chicken livers and pork seasoned with brandy, chives, peppercorns and pistachi. To follow, perhaps scampi thermidor or a pork fillet saute in onions, apricots, brandy, cream and crushed peppercorns. For the vegetarian, asparagus hollandaise should appeal. An Usher's house, so real ale is represented by Usher's Best and Ruddle's Best. Children's meals are available.

Children are welcome.
Dogs too — in the public bar.

BRATTON — THE DUKE

The Westbury White Horse on the north-western edge of Salisbury Plains does not have the antiquity or reputation of the attenuated figure in Berkshire, but is probably the best known in Wiltshire as it stands above the lowland vale between Frome and Devizes. It is reached by any of the three routes here and lies just below the ancient earthworks of Bratton Camp. Enjoy also the peaceful setting of the church tucked in a combe on the edge of, and almost separate from, the village. The occasional crump of artillery is a reminder that the ridge track follows the edge of the Imber ranges, so don't stray.

Walk 1	**2 miles**	**Parts A B E**
Walk 2	**3½ miles**	**Parts A C E**
Walk 3	**5 miles**	**Parts D E**

A **TR** and **X** to *The Butts* opposite. Ahead **FR** to the last house and immediately **TL** down a narrow path, over a bridge, to the church.

B Just beyond the church **TR** over a stile and climb across the hillside to **X** another stile above. **CR** to *Bratton Camp.*

C Just beyond the church **X** a stile and follow the path up the hillside to **X** another stile above. Continue ahead to **X** a stile by a gate next to a barn and onto the broad ridge track. **TR** and, before the track curves left, again **TR** to *Bratton Camp.*

D **TL** along the road for about ½ mile. Just before the village of *Edington.* **TR**, before a white cottage, up a broad track signed *The Plain.* The path meanders above a reservoir up to *Edington Hill* before straightening out to a gentle descent. Pass through 2 gates to eventually arrive at an army gatepost. Sharply **TR** along the approach road and shortly **TL** along the ridge track. Almost 2 miles on, where the track curves left, **TR** to *Bratton Camp.*

E From *Bratton Camp* follow the road down to *Bratton.* As it curves left, go straight on along a path which shortly crosses a driveway and enters *The Butts* from the top end. Pass the houses and **CL** down to the pub.

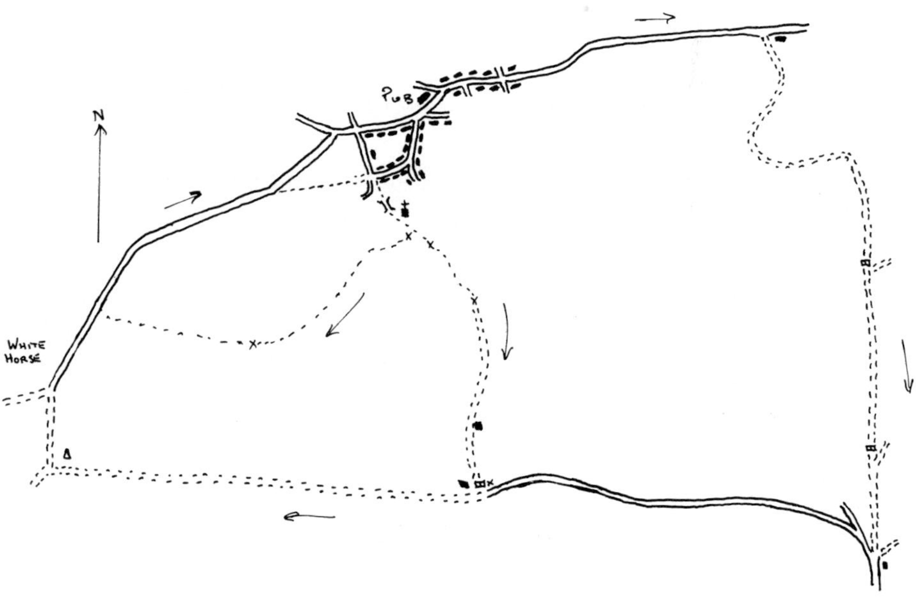

Westbury White Horse, Bratton

Dundas aqueduct, Winsley

O.S. MAP NO. 173 : 976 727

The inn is situated at the corner of a cross roads above the village. Take any of the roads to the north off the A4 between Chippenham and Calne.
The inn has lay-by type parking space, otherwise park around the green out front.

HOURS:	Sunday	12.00 - 2.30	:	7.00 - 10.30
	Weekdays	11.30 - 2.30	:	7.00 - 11.00
	Saturday	11.30 - 2.30	:	7.00 - 11.00

N.B. Closed Wednesday until 7.00

This is an eighteenth century Cotswold stone and tile building with exterior seating on the pleasant green in front, and in a garden and patio to one side. There are two bars with open log fires. Following a long walk, choose between a pint of Bass, Archer's Best, or Wadworth's 6X — Old Timer is kept in winter. I think Mr and Mrs Pitt would agree that food is not a speciality. There is no restaurant service and bar snacks are available only at lunchtimes.

On a warm day it can be most relaxing to sit or lie in the garden with your favourite pint, enjoying the view south towards Bowood.

Children are allowed in at lunchtime.
Dogs are welcome at any time.

Here is a group of walks which includes a number of features of interest and a variety of distances in six combinations. There is a nature trail along a disused railway line beside the River Mardon (May-Sept only), and a monument erected by the Marquis of Lansdown to Maud Heath, a medieval rambler and philanthropist who funded a much-needed causeway across low-lying land liable to flooding between Bremhill and Chippenham. For example, Walk 1 has the nature trail but not the monument, whereas Walk 2 reverses this. Perhaps a tortuous schema, yet hopefully useful.

Walk 1	**3 miles**	**Parts A B**
Walk 2	**3 miles**	**Parts D E G H K**
Walk 3	**3½ miles**	**Parts D E G J K**
Walk 4	**4½ miles**	**Parts A C E F**
Walk 5	**5 miles**	**Parts A C E G H K**
Walk 6	**5½ miles**	**Parts A C E G J K**

From the inn **TL** past the car park and walk down the lane.

A Eventually, this lane crosses a bridge over a disused railway line which is now a nature trail. **TR** to follow its course round to the next road bridge. Sharply **TL** up to a metal gate and out onto a road. **TR** and **X** the bridge. Continue along the road and **FR** at a junction.

B Go up to a crossroads about 1 mile ahead and **TR** for the inn.

C About ¾ mile ahead look for a new bungalow just past an old stone farmhouse on the left. About 100 yards beyond, opposite a path into the wood on the right, **TL** through a metal gate.

D Just before a bungalow on the right, **TR** through a metal gate into a field. **BR** up between 2 woods. Go through a wooden gate into the next field. **X** to the **URH** corner and enter the wood through a small wooden gate. Shortly exit onto a road and go through the metal gate opposite.

E Keeping close to the wire fence on the left, **X** to the far side and **TR** along a broad path. Stay on this path to pass through 4 metal gates, the last to the left of a house, and onto a road. **X** the stile next to the metal gate opposite. Ahead is the monument.

F Return to the road and **TL.** Ahead is a T-junction. **TR** along the road, over a crossroads, and back to the inn.

G Beyond the monument, on the edge of the hill, is a metal gate into the next field. Go through and, ignoring the small wooden gate to the left, approach another small wooden gate ahead. Pass into the next field and, keeping left, **X** to a stile and metal gate.

H Remaining in the same field, **TR** along the track and onto a road. Go down the road, past a turning to the left, to **TR** through a metal gate just beyond 2 houses on either side of the road.

J **X** the stile and go straight on through a series of metal and wooden gates onto a road. *(Lyneham airfield is on the hill ahead)*. Go through a metal gate opposite and **X** to a wooden gate in the centre of the far side. Pass over the small wooden bridge in front and through to **TR** along the hedge. Pass above a farm and through a gap in the hedge ahead. Immediately **X** a plank over a stream and go up to a wooden gate ahead. Go through to the next field and through a wire gate to the left of a house and next to a wooden shed. **X** the road and go through the metal gate opposite.

K **BL** over the brow of the hill, towards the church, and down to go through a metal gate in the **LH** hedge. Continue down to a metal gate in the middle of the far hedge. Go through onto a road. **TR** up to the village cross. **TL** through the churchyard and out through a small metal gate at the back. **BL,** then **CR** round the houses to the right. **X** a stile and continue along the ridge to a metal gate next to a cottage ahead. Go through to the inn.

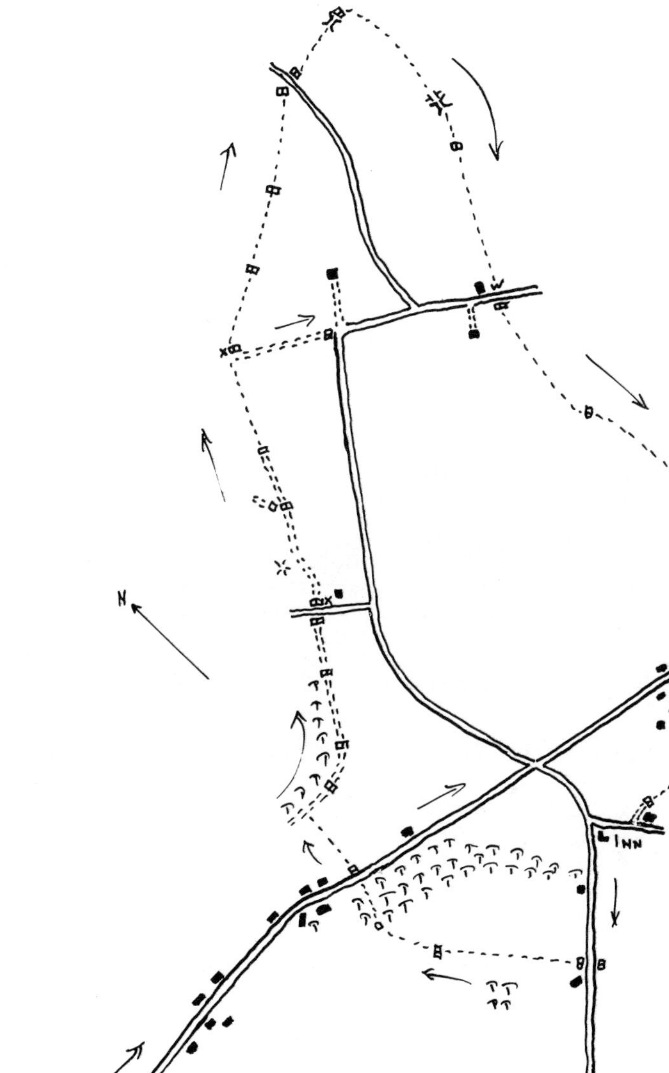
N
INN
W

O.S. MAP NO. 184 (also 174) : 254 538

From the south turn right, from the north turn left, at Collingbourne Ducis on the A338, up a minor road to Cadley. The inn is at a crossroads about a mile from Collingbourne Ducis. Park at the front, side or rear.

HOURS:	Sunday	12.00 - 3.00	:	7.00 - 10.30
	Weekdays	11.00 - 3.00	:	6.30 - 11.00
	Saturday	11.00 - 3.00	:	6.30 - 11.00

N.B. Catering until 2.00 and again until 9.30.

Apparently, The Shears takes its name from the fact that sheep were sheared here, the last inn before market at Weyhill near Andover. Originally a sixteenth century coaching inn of brick and flint with a thatched roof, a recent extension of old bricks and timbers now gives a total accommodation of bar, lounge and restaurant.

Mr Bullock, the present owner, was awarded Les Routiers 'Pub of the Year' in 1988 at his previous establishment. Certainly, the emphasis here is on comfort and food of a high standard. The menu changes daily and the fresh produce is freshly cooked with, Mr Bullock proudly told me, not a chip in sight. Although children's meals are not provided, vegetarian dishes are available by arrangement.

Three real ales are kept: Wadworth's 6X, Greene King's Abbott Ale and Usher's Best.

There is en suite accommodation for weekend breaks and longer stays.

Children are welcome.
Dogs also.

The walks here are pleasant, fairly easy and straightforward, passing through woodland and hilltop pasture and arable land. Coldridge Wood is a young beech enclosure with wild primroses in abundance. However, the imagination may also be stimulated by the place names. Walk through Gammon's Farm and New Zealand — a collection of farm buildings — over Mount Cowdown, Bauks Hill and Chute Down.

Walk 1	**3½ miles**	**Parts A B**
Walk 2	**5½ miles**	**Parts A C D**
Walk 3	**6 miles**	**Parts A C E**

A From the car park **TL** along the lane to shortly **FL** through a metal gate onto a bridleway. As it approaches a copse **FR** along a path on the edge of the copse. Ahead exit through a metal gate onto a partially metalled track. **TR** up to a junction with another track.

B **TR** into the wood and shortly **FR** to the wood's edge. Continue along the edge of the wood on a narrow path and eventually **TR** along a grassy track to the inn.

C **CL** to pass through *Gammon's Farm*, then just beyond power lines **TR** through a metal gate into a field. **X** to a small wooden gate and continue along the inner edge of a small wood. Exit through *New Zealand* on a gravel track. Where this curves left, go straight on along a grassy track between trees. Shortly, look carefully for a gap and a pair of metal gates on the **R.** Go through and **BL** along the edge of a field. At the far end **BL** through a metal gate onto a lane. Continue along the lane, past a white house and go through a large metal gate. Shortly pass through a small wooden gate and continue ahead along the edge of a field. Near the far end **BL** through a spinney, then **TR** along a gravel track.

D **CR** downhill to **TL** through a pair of metal gates below. **TR** straight up the far hill, keeping close to the wood on the right. At the top go through a metal gate into *Collingbourne Wood* and on over a junction with a metalled track to the far edge of the wood. Here, at a T-junction with a path, **TL** between the edge of the wood and a field. At the end of the field **TR** along a grassy track to the inn.

E As the track curves right, go straight on through a metal gate. Approach *Coldridge Wood* ahead to **X** a stile by a wooden gate and, keeping the wood to the left, continue along a grassy track on an earthwork embankment. Shortly the track enters the wood, then **FR** down to a junction. Go straight on to the bottom to join another track from the right. **TL** along it and immediately **TR** onto a metalled track. Eventually, where this curves left, go straight ahead along a grassy track to the inn.

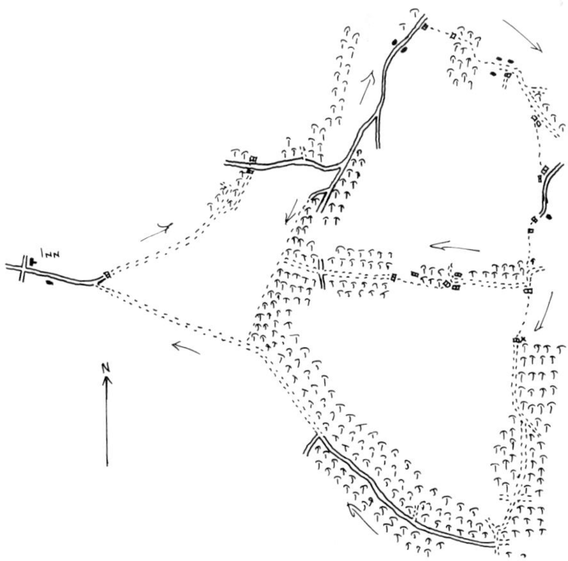

O.S. MAP NO. 173 : 040 617

Take the A361 from Devizes towards Swindon. On the outskirts of the town, about one mile from the centre, turn right along a minor road over the Kennet and Avon canal and take the first right again on entering the village of Coate.
Ample parking is provided.

HOURS:	Sunday	12.00 - 3.00	:	7.00 - 10.30
	Weekdays	12.00 - 2.00	:	5.00 - 11.00
	Saturday	11.00 - 3.00	:	6.30 - 11.00

N.B. Closed Thursday until 5.00

This brick and slate Wadworth's house does not go in for frills. Put simply, there is no food and the lounge might be considered full with a half dozen visitors standing, or sitting on the homely furniture. However, the warmth, friendliness and sheer enthusiasm of its landlady, Mrs Baston-Coultiss, and local regulars make it shine out. Both she and husband Tony are members of CAMRA and The Society for the Preservation of Beers from the Wood. "Ask for lager at your peril", she warned me. (As a parenthetical aside to the lager drinkers in my audience I should, perhaps, mention that Harp is on draught here). Tony is also an active steam railway enthusiast.

Apart from the lounge there is a larger public bar decorated with photographs of shire horses and some fifteen years of carnival float entries, together with an original oil painting of a narrow guage steam locomotive. There is also a skittle alley cum family room and a large garden. Quench your thirst with a pint of 6X, IPA or, occasionally, Old Timer.

Children and dogs, like the rest of creation, are welcome here.

The northern edge of the Vale of Pewsey consists of some of the finest hills in the county. Many walks climb and pass along Milk Hill, Tan Hill, Morgan's Hill. However, from Coate I have preferred three walks that view them from the valley itself. Only Walk 1 has a short climb over the minor outlier of Etchilhampton Hill, the others keep to lowland pasture, arable land and different sections of the Kennet and Avon canal.

Walk 1	**3 miles**	**Part A**
Walk 2	**4 miles**	**Parts B D**
Walk 3	**5 miles**	**Parts C D**

A **TR** directly along a broad track and **TL** about 1 mile ahead. Approach *Etchilhampton Hill* ahead to **TL** through a gate up to the triangulation point on top. Continue down to a metal gate onto a road. **TL** to *Coate* and the inn.

B **TR** directly along a broad track and **TR** about 1 mile ahead. Go over a low hill to the road beyond. **TL** to the canal and **TR** along the near bank. Just over 1 mile ahead pass beneath power lines and immediately **TR** up the bank onto a road. **TR** to a T-junction and **TR** through a metal gate into a field.

C **TL** to the main village street, then **TR** to the last bungalow. **TL** along the track beside it to a junction. Go straight on through a double metal gate towards power lines. Pass through a metal gate into a field and continue along, keeping close to the hedge on the left. Go through a wire gate into the next field. Go on to **X** a double stile and bridge over a stream. Immediately **BL** under the power lines to **X** another bridge over another stream. Go towards *All Cannings* church over 3 wooden fences. After the third **TR** along the hedge and follow the field boundary along the edge of the village and fully round to the canal. **TL** along the bank. At the third bridge exit onto a road and **TL** through the village of Horton. On the outskirts **TL** again along a lane and at a T-junction **TR** under power lines to another T-junction with a road ahead. Go through a metal gate opposite into a field.

D **TL,** go through a gap in a wire fence and drop down to **X** a stile in the middle of the far hedge. Go on to **X** a tree trunk over a stream. Ahead pass between a farm to the right and cottages to the left. Continue to the far metal gate out onto a lane. **TL** and then immediately **TR** at a T-junction along another lane to the inn.

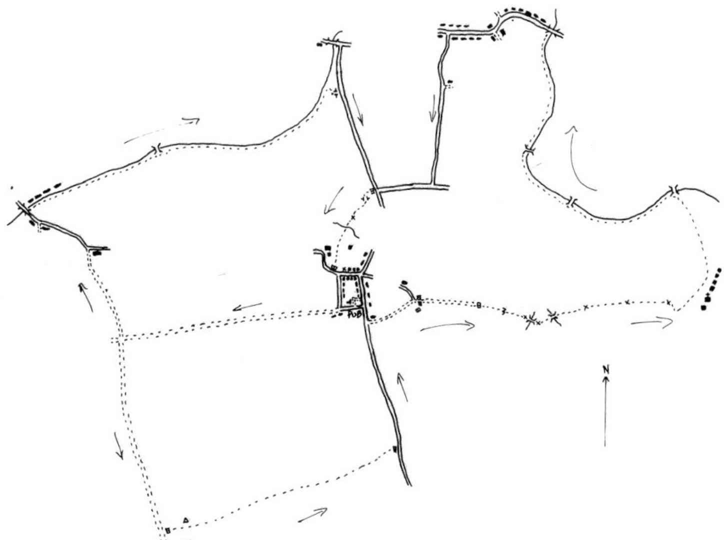

O.S. MAP NO. 183 : 813 457

The pub is on the A362 midway between Warminster and Frome.
There is an ample car park here.

HOURS:	Sunday	12.00 - 3.00	:	7.00 - 10.30
	Weekdays	11.00 - 3.00	:	6.00 - 11.00
	Saturday	11.00 - 3.00	:	6.00 - 11.00

The White Hart is putatively three hundred years old and has been part of the Longleat estate for all that time, although originally a brewery. The single bar with much brasswork and timber in evidence is complemented by a separate restaurant. The bar also boasts a stuffed owl overlooking proceedings from its glass case. Mr Beynon, the owner, has been fascinated by owls for many years, has studied them and collects almost anything connected with them. There is a possibility that the hen barn owl he owns may be trained to reside in the bar.

The pub keeps four regular ales — Palmer's Best, Eldridge Pope's Royal Oak, Wadworth's 6X, and Bass — along with two guest ales. Numerous blackboards denote the regularly changing fare of bar snacks and restaurant meals. Vegetarians are adequately catered for and children's meals are available.

Children are, of course, allowed in the restaurant.
Yet no dogs, please.

Cley Hill, like the more famous Silbury Hill, is an enormous earthwork. Folklore extends the similarity. According to local legends both are the result of the devil dropping a huge sackful of earth while on his way to dump it on a nearby town whose inhabitants had irritated him. Thus Cley Hill was originally destined for Devizes, Silbury Hill for Marlborough. It is Cley Hill that is the focus of this walk. Unfortunately, for a circular walk the only access is from the busy Warminster to Frome road, although it has been possible to reduce use of this to some 300 yards.

Walk 5½ miles

TL along the minor road beside the pub. Where it bears right **TL** by a house *Hill Rising* up a stony track which quickly becomes a narrow path. As the path ahead curves left **BR** over a stile into a field. **TL** to **X** a stile onto a lane. **TL** and shortly **TR** over a stile by a wooden gate into a field. Go directly down the steep slope to **X** a stile to the right of the cottage below. Exit onto a lane junction. Go ahead to **CL** round to another T-junction. **TR** up a stony track. Just before it enters a wood **TL** over a stile by a metal gate. **X** another stile ahead and go along the edge of a fir copse. **X** a stile and **TR** along the edge of the field to **X** another stile in the centre of the **RH** side. Go straight ahead through a gap in the hedge onto a stony track. **TL** down to a road junction. Continue to the main road, **TR** up to the entrance to *Cley Hill* and **TL**.

Along the approach path **TR** and immediately **L** to the hill. Return to this point and **TL** along a path between and below 2 fields. Exit, keeping to the left of a wire fence, and go on to pass through the **LH** metal gate ahead. **BL** towards the *Warminster by-pass* to go through another metal gate onto a metalled track beside it. **TL** to go through another metal gate and immediately **BL** through yet another metal gate. Follow the track, which eventually becomes a narrow path along the edge of a wood. Exit through a metal gate into a field. Continue down to pass a farm through a succession of 3 metal gates. Exit onto a lane. Go along to a T-junction and continue along the drive opposite. **TR** past the front of a stone cottage and immediately **TL** through a metal gate. Go along a track, through 2 metal gates, then into a field. Keeping to the left of a wire fence, continue ahead to exit just left of houses onto a lane. Follow the lane to a road and **CL** along the road to **TR** over a stile by a metal gate just before houses. Go ahead and shortly **BL** across a succession of 4 stiles to the main road. **TR** to the pub.

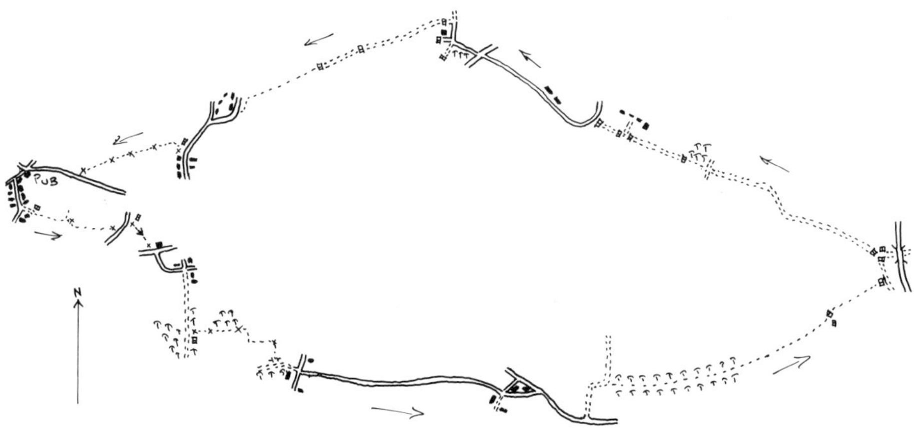

CORTON **THE DOVE**

O.S. MAP NO. 184 : 935 405

From the west, turn right off the A36 at Heytesbury to Tytherington, then turn left to Corton. From the east, turn left at Upton Lovell off the A36, cross the river and turn right for Corton. The pub is almost hidden at the west end of the village, tucked in between the middle and left-hand fork of a triple-forked junction.
The pub has space for about twenty cars, otherwise use the adjacent lanes.

HOURS:	Sunday	12.00 - 2.30	:	CLOSED
	Weekdays	11.00 - 2.30	:	6.00 - 11.00
	Saturday	11.00 - 2.30	:	6.00 - 11.00

N.B. Closed Sunday evening and all day Monday.

Built about 1850, this Usher's house was The New Inn until 1969 when it became The Dove from the dovecote on the front wall. It has one bar and a separate restaurant. Imaginatively decorated in French Cape style, it has something of the feeling of a private residence. Perhaps this explains why it possesses one of the few outside toilets to have central heating — and very comfortable too. So is the delightful garden.

The food here has developed such a reputation that a book of recipes is available at the bar — Balinese Spiced Fish took my fancy. Unfortunately the only real ale is Usher's Best. Also the pub is about to change hands.

Children are, of course, allowed in the restaurant.
Dogs in the bar only.
(Since writing the above I have heard that The Dove has been acquired by Belhaven Brewery of East Lothian, part of Control Securities PLC. Future plans remain unclear at the time of writing, though expect at least the beer to change).

CORTON — THE DOVE

A short amble across meadows and the Southampton to Bristol railway line takes you along the River Wylye, through the villages of Knook and Upton Lovell. Flat and easy. In the opposite direction a longer walk passes through fields and a wood on the ridge above the valley. Link the two together for an even longer walk, though Part B is then more logically done in reverse. In this case I suggest you first become more familiar with it as a crucial junction is perhaps rather difficult to spot first time around.

Walk 1	**3 miles**	**Part A**
Walk 2	**6½ miles**	**Part B**

A From the pub **TR** up to the road. Immediately **TR** over a stile into a field. **X** the field and stile ahead, past greenhouses, to **X** another stile by a metal gate. Proceed to another stile part way along the field and **X** into the adjacent field. Go on to **X** yet another stile, then through the railway arch ahead. **TL** over a stile into the field beside the railway. Keeping close to the hedge on the right, pass through a wire gate and **BR** along a track to a metal gate onto a lane. Go on to follow the lane round a horseshoe bend. Follow the track past the farmhouse, through a first metal gate and on to a second. Do not go through, but **TR** along the far edge of this field towards a cottage ahead. Go straight over a broad track to **BR** along the river bank. **X** a stile and **TL** over a bridge. **BR** onto a track and follow it round past Knook church. Here **TR** along a lane, then **FR** along a track. Go through 2 metal gates, **X** a field, and on through a metal gate beside a stone house. Go ahead to a lane. Walk through *Upton Lovell* to **TR** by a chestnut tree along a track to the river. Shortly **FL** along the path, over a bridge and stile into a field. Go on, through a metal gate, then **TL** to **X** a stile and on to carefully **X** the railway line. Continue along to a lane and **TL** through the village to *The Dove.*

B **TR** up to the road and along it for about ½ mile. Shortly after an S-bend, **TL** up a long gently-winding track and eventually **CR** into a field. Keeping close to the wire fence on the right, go up to the edge of the wood above to pass through a gap in a fence and onto a track which soon joins a much broader track following the line of the ridge through the wood. **TL** and follow this broad track for some way to **CL** and meander out of the wood just over a mile ahead. Eventually, soon after a barn to the left, **TL** at a junction with a metalled track and continue to a junction with another metalled track. **TR** and immediately **TL** down a steep stony track to the road below. Directly opposite is a narrow path down to the pub.

Nockett's Hill from Derry Hill

O.S. MAP NO. 173 : 956 706

The pub is on the A342 a half mile south of the junction with the A4 between Chippenham and Calne, standing opposite Golden Gates and the turning to Bowood House.
There is sufficient parking space at the pub and in a nearby lay-by.

HOURS:	Sunday	12.00 - 2.30	:	7.00 - 10.30
	Weekdays	11.00 - 2.30	:	6.00 - 11.00
	Saturday	11.00 - 2.30	:	6.00 - 11.00

N.B. The restaurant serves Sunday from 6.30 - 9.30 and weekdays from 6.30 - 10.00

This imposing limestone Wadworth's house is run by Mike and Yvonne Freegard and Mrs Jones who have a combined experience in the licensed trade of seventy-five years. Yvonne has lived here all her life — her parents ran it — and her hobby of cake-making is evident on the menu. Mike is a keen photographer and some of his work graces the bar, particularly a sunset view from the pub. He tells me a strong smell of yeast heralds the presence of the ghost of the baker from a once adjacent bakery.

The bar, the lounge with its leaded windows and chintz, and the restaurant are all warm and comfortable. All food, including bar snacks, is home-made, from the prawn caprice (prawns in seafood sauce with melon) to the pheasant in madeira and to the flambe medallions of pork in sherry. Both children's meals and vegetarian dishes are available separately. Choose your refreshment from 6X, IPA, or Farmer's Glory. In the winter Old Timer is added, while in summer Bulmer's Medium cider is kept.

Children can come into the restaurant.
Dogs in the bar.

Derry Hill, Nocketts Hill and Bowden Hill south-east of Chippenham overlook the clay vale in which it lies and through which runs the Avon. All are included on the longer walk which passes along the bank to cross the river at Reybridge before entering Lacock. It recrosses the river by the abbey to climb up to Bowden Park from where there is a pleasant view back over the abbey to the village and beyond. At the top of Bowden Park is a cemetery for pets. If you wish, why not visit the abbey and the Fox-Talbot photographic museum in Lacock, and Bowood House and gardens on Derry Hill. Of course, it would be quite possible to commence the longer route at Lacock. Yet it would then lack a focus, an objective, while adding to the perennial parking problem.

In 1574 the daughter of the abbey owner so despaired of being allowed to marry her beloved that she leapt from the battlements. Her billowing petticoats helped to save her. Appropriately enough so did the beloved who almost died when she landed on top of him. Her father promptly gave permission and his blessing.

Walk 1	**2½ miles**	**Parts A B D**
Walk 2	**7 miles**	**Parts A C D**

A Carefully **BR** over the main road to **TR** along a narrow path between hedges alongside a house. Drop directly down over 3 stiles in quick succession and continue to drop directly down to a 4th in a hedge below. **X** a bridge over the stream at the bottom, then make way to the far hedge above. Look carefully for a wire gate into the next field. Continue upwards, passing close to a copse on the right, towards a white cottage ahead. Pass through 2 metal gates to the lane by the cottage. Go on between the cottage and a bungalow to the left to pass through a metal gate. Ahead are 2 narrow paths to the left.

B **BL** along the first narrow path, past a chalet to the left above, through a gap in a hedge into the next field. In the **ULH** corner **X** a wooden frame over a ditch and a stone stile in a wire fence into the next field. Go along the edge of a copse to the left to join a metalled track traversing the centre of the field. **TL** up this track through the copse. It meanders up to a hedge where it turns right and straightens out. However, **TL** along this hedge.

C **BL** along the second narrow path, **X** a wooden fence in the hedge ahead and **BR** across a metalled track to pass through a metal gate into the next field. Go ahead through the next metal gate in the far hedge and go on to a spinney on the far side. Go through to **X** a stile into the field beyond. Go on to **X** another stile by a metal gate. Shortly **TR** before a decrepit brick bridge to go through 2 small wooden gates into the next field. Continue above the river to **X** a stile into a spinney and out into the field beyond. At the far end **BL** through a wire gate into the adjacent field. Slightly **BR** to a pair of metal stiles and along a narrow path between fences. **X** another metal stile onto a lane. **X** the metal stile opposite and **BL** across the field to **X** another stile by a bridge. Exit onto a road and **TR** over the bridge. **TL** and, as the road turns right, continue ahead up an asphalt path, through a small wooden gate. Continue towards a radio mast and exit through a small wooden gate onto a lane. **TL** down to *Lacock.*

Return along the road past the abbey. **TL** over a stone stile set in the stone wall on the far side of the river. **X** the meadow directly to a stile in the far hedge. **X** into the field beyond and **BR** to the **RH** corner to **TR** through a wire gate into the next field. Ahead **X** a stile onto a lane. **BL** over the grass to go up a narrow path between fields. Shortly **TR** over a stile into a field. **TL** and go through a large metal gate. Keeping close to the hedge on the left, go up to and along the edge of the wood. Above **TL** through a wooden gate and continue up to **X** a stile by another wooden gate. **CL** along the edge of the wood to **X** a stile and **TL** to shortly go through a small wooden gate into and through a copse. **X** a stile into the field beyond. Follow the fence on the left to **X** another stile. Pass along a paddock fence, then at the end **TR** over a stile and immediately over another into the field beyond. **BR** to pass through a metal gate onto a lane. **TL**, then **TR** along a track towards *Ash Hill Farm*. As the track curves left below, continue ahead along the hedge.

D At the end of the hedge descend to **X** a stile into the next field. Make way to the far hedge and drop down to a small wooden gate onto a narrow path between fields. This is the head of an increasingly steep gully and becomes increasingly wooded, though the path remains level above it. Eventually a field appears to the right in a broad gap in the wood below. Here **TR** to the **LLH** corner and turn left through a wooden gate to **CR** through a metal gate. Immediately **TL** through a gap in a hedge. Go on, the wood now to the left, to **X** a double wire fence in a gap in the hedge ahead. **BR** to the **RH** side of the next field to pass through a wooden gate, then **BL** to a small barn and on through the metal gate behind. Shortly **TR** over a stile in the hedge to the right *(the 4th of the beginning of Part A)* up to the pub.

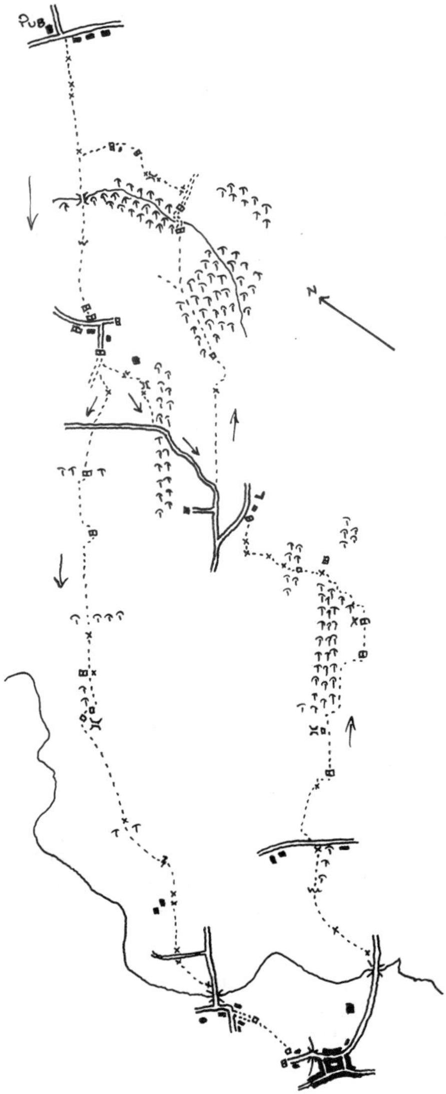

Old Wardour Castle, Ansty

Whitesheet Hill, Little Knoll and Long Knoll from Brimsdown Hill, Horningsham

O.S. MAP NO. 184 : 993 243

Take the A30 south-west from Wilton. After Fovant, take the first left over the downs to Fifield Babant, then turn right for Ebbesbourne Wake. The inn is in the village below the church.
There is limited parking space on the premises and most folk park along the village.

HOURS:	Sunday	12.00 - 3.00	:	7.00 - 10.30
	Weekdays	12.00 - 2.30	:	7.00 - 10.30
	Saturday	11.30 - 2.30	:	7.00 - 11.00

N.B. Friday evening is extended to 11.00.
Summer times too may be extended. The restaurant is closed on Monday.

Built at the end of the eighteenth century, this stone and brick building is appropriately run by the Bath family, a name which has been in the village for over five hundred years. However, Anthony and Pat have been at The Horseshoe Inn for a mere sixteen years. The two bars are imaginatively decorated with old tools and artifacts connected with rural workmanship. With open fireplaces the atmosphere is snug and cosy. I felt very comfortable here, and not only because I could vary my refreshment between Wadworth's 6X, Bunce's Best, Adnam's Broadside — the three regular beers — and Thatcher's Farm cider. Additional guest beers are 'on' during winter.

Besides the bar snacks, plenty of good home-cooked food may be enjoyed in the separate dining-room. Vegetarian meals are available, though children's meals are not.

Neither children or dogs are allowed on the premises.

A leisurely stroll of 10½ miles over chalk downs and across the Ebble valley between also takes in the neighbouring villages of Alvediston and Bowerchalke. The triangulation point on the northern ridge provides an oblique view of regimental insignia cut into the same chalk hills to the east, and reminders of other walks (Ansty, page 13) are the maypole below and the conifer plantation above Old Wardour Castle to the north-west. On the southern ridge is another part of the Ox Drove (Tollard Royal, page 87). Altogether a peaceful route as some combes seem to retain a feeling of isolation.

Walk 1	**3½ miles**	**Parts A B**
Walk 2	**5½ miles**	**Parts A C D**
Walk 3	**10½ miles**	**Parts A C E**

A **TR**, then **FL** down a lane, past cottages, to a metal gate on the right as the lane curves left. **TR** along a narrow path between wire fences, **X** a wooden bridge, and **TL** over a stile into a field. **X** up to a stile just beyond the line of trees in the **RH** hedge. **TL** along the lane and immediately **TR** over a stile before the house ahead. Go up the narrow path and over another stile into a field. Shortly, **TR** through a small wooden gate. **TL**, now with the fence to the left. **TR** at the top, the fence still to the left. Go down to a broad gap in this fence, **TL** and immediately **TR** through a metal gate. Go on, keeping the wire fence to the right. At the end of the fence **TL** down and across to a metal gate to the right of a line of trees. Go through and up the hill. **BL**, the valley to the left, a wire fence to the right. Go through a gap in a wire fence ahead towards a line of trees across the valley head. **BR** through the far end of the trees up to a metal gate and onto a junction of broad tracks. Go straight on up to the top, **TL** and shortly go through a metal gate onto the ridge track. **TL** and immediately **TR** between 2 fields. Go through a metal gate and on to **FL** along a wire fence, then sharp **L** through a metal gate to a triangulation point. Ahead is the ridge track again.

B **X** this track to go down another broad track to the road below. Go past *West End Cottage*, over a bridge and immediately **TL** along a lane. **FL** to the inn.

C **TR** along the ridge track. About 1 mile ahead, just beyond where the track briefly divides, **TL** over a stile. **BR** across the head of the combe and go along the **RH** ridge. **X** a stile next to a metal gate and **X** a field to another stile by a wooden gate. **X** the road to continue down the track opposite. Pass 2 houses and **TL** along a narrow path by a wire fence. Go through a wooden gate, continue across a field to a stile ahead, and onto a road.

D Go through the metal gate opposite and **BR** across the grass. Go through a wooden gate and **X** to another wooden gate ahead. Go through, along the gravel track to the road. **TR** over a bridge and immediately **TL** along the lane. **FL** to the inn.

E **TR** down the road to a T-junction. **TR** again then **L** up a lane to *Elcombe Farm*. Continue past the farm up to the *Ox Drove* track above. **TL** along the track, following it onto and along a road, to **TL** through a metal gate past a pair of barns. **TL** again and go along a path round a copse. Drop down over the brow of the hill to the bottom. Go through a gap in a wire fence and **BL**, a wire fence to the left, round the hill to the right. *(Ahead where the wire fence gives way to a wooden paddock fence I am assured access will be made available through the wire boundary fences).* Continue round the hill, through a wooden gate, and **TR** along a metalled track. Go through another wooden gate, through farm buildings, past houses, and onto a road. Go along the road to a T-junction. **TL** along the gravel track opposite, past a farm to the right, and onto a path to a broad track. **TL** along the track which turns **R** towards a field at the end. **TL**, keeping the hedgerow to the left, then at the end of the field **TR** up to a small wooden gate on the hilltop. Go through and go round to another small wooden gate opposite. Pass through into a spinney and out through another small wooden gate into the field beyond. Similarly, **X** to another small wooden gate and beyond towards a white house and farm buildings. Go through a wire gate and along the left hand side of the wire fence ahead. **TR** through a large wire gate, go through the farmyard and onto a broad track. **TR** along the track, then **TL** over the hilltop down to the road. **TR**, then **FR** to the inn.

O.S. MAP NO. 173 : 842 248

The pub is just off the main A420. Turn left into the village about five miles west of Chippenham.
A large parking area lies over the brook just beyond the pub.

HOURS:	Sunday	12.00 - 3.00	:	7.00 - 10.30
	Weekdays	11.00 - 3.00	:	6.00 - 11.00
	Saturday	11.00	———	11.00

The White Hart, beautifully set by a trout stream in a steep-sided valley, is a listed building of Cotswold stone and has been an inn since 1553. Take your ease outside by By Brook in the summer — winter too, if you wish. If not, the Cotswold stone and beamed interior with its log fires will be cosy enough. Apart from the single bar there is a buttery and a restaurant.

I could say that food is a special consideration here. It is, with a wide variety of bar snacks (huge steak and kidney pies) which includes provision for children and vegetarians. Yet the choice of food is matched by the choice of real ales: Bass, Wadworth's 6X, Fuller's ESB and London Pride, Badger Best and Tanglefoot, Ruddle's Best, Marston's Pedigree, Smiles' Exhibition, and Greene King's Abbott Ale. There is also West Country Traditional scrumpy.

Bill Futcher, the landlord, was twenty-four years in the Royal Navy as a frogman and bomb disposal expert, subsequently spending twelve years with a major oil company.

Children are allowed on the premises.
So too are dogs.

Walks in two quite different directions follow a similar pattern and offer a comparison of two particularly charming Cotswold villages. A brief, steep ascent from the pub apart, the shortest walk is all very easy and amiable as it passes the church at Slaughterford and returns along the banks of By Brook — one of the shortest walks in this collection. The longer walks similarly have an early ascent of a hillside before steadily dropping down to the award-winning Castle Combe, again returning along the banks of By Brook after it has flowed through and out of the village. Some very pretty scenery here in what is really a narrow and secluded valley.

FORD — THE WHITE HART

Walk 1	**1½ miles**	**Part A**
Walk 2	**2½ miles**	**Parts B C E**
Walk 3	**4 miles**	**Parts B D E**

A **TL**, **X** the bridge and **FR** up a steep lane to *Slaughterford*. Opposite a T-junction **X** a stile into a field, pass the church, and beyond exit through a metal gate onto a lane. Go down to where the lane turns left. Here **TR** after the last cottage over a stile by a metal gate. Go on to **X** a bridge over the brook and continue along to shortly **TR** over a sluice gate back to the other bank. **BL** along the bank to **X** a stile in a wire fence. Shortly **X** the brook over a pair of stiles and a bridge. Continue to a bridge by the confluence with a small stream. **TL** past a paddock to **X** a stile by a wooden gate onto a road. **TR** to the pub.

B **TR** to the road and again **TR** to the main road. Carefully **X** over and **TR** to a drive between houses just before the road to *Castle Combe*. **TL** up this drive to **X** a stile and **TR** along a narrow path into a steeply-sided wood. **X** a pair of stiles and bridge to climb the opposite hillside. **BL** along a path below the ridge to **X** a stile by a wooden gate. Ahead go through another wooden gate onto a road junction. **FL** along the upper road and shortly **TR** over a stile in a wire fence. Continue to another stile and exit onto the lower road. **TL** to *Castle Combe*.

C On entering the village notice a stone footbridge over the brook. **TR** over this bridge *(or enter the village and return to this point)*, then **TR** again along the far bank to **X** a stone stile by a metal gate. Continue above the bank for about ½ mile.

D As the road climbs out of the village **BR** up a narrow path towards a wood above. Go through a kissing gate to merge with a bridlepath above. Immediately **TR** along a broad grassy path above the previous path. Follow this above the wood, round and, eventually, down to merge with another path following the course of the brook.

E Look for a broken stone wall on the right. Here **TR** down a path to the brook and shortly **X** a bridge to the far bank by a stone cottage. **TL** along the bank to **X** 2 bridges over ditches, the second about a ½ mile on. Immediately **X** a stile by a metal gate. **TR** up a broad track, **FR** at a house ahead, and pass through a wooden gate beyond. Continue above the brook and **FL** to **X** a stile onto a road. **TL** down to *Ford*.

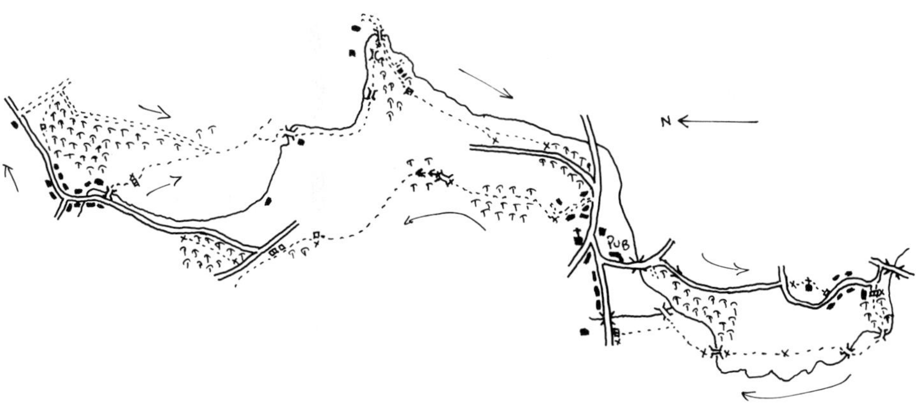

O.S. MAP NO. 184 : 077 355

From Wilton, take the minor road north for about three miles. Alternatively, from the A36 turn left at Stoford about three miles north of Wilton.
Use the pub car park or the lanes.

This is an Usher's house, keeping Usher's Best and Ruddle's Best. One main bar of dark oak beams and panelling has an adjacent lounge area comfortably furnished with upholstered seating, including a leather sofa. There is a separate dining area. The specialities here seem to be a range of ploughman's (Wiltshire Lad with cheddar and ham, Cavalryman's with stilton and sausage, King Ploughman's with assorted cheeses) and chocolate-based desserts (Death-by-Chocolate, Chocolate Bomb, chocolate nut sundae, chocolate fudge cake). I rather go for the treacle roly-poly. Either as starter or main course are giant green-lipped mussels with garlic bread. A self-serve salad bar is available.

Similar to the long walk from Corton, this walk too climbs easily above the Wylye valley to pass through Grovely Wood and back again. It affords the simple pleasures of open pasture, mixed woodland and fine views of the valley, together with a glimpse of the distant Salisbury cathedral spire. There is a tradition that on Oak Apple Day, May 29th, the villagers gather wood from Grovely Wood and, after decorating their homes with green oak boughs, go to Salisbury to dance outside the cathedral. This tradition is represented in the pub sign.

Walk 4 miles

TR and go under the railway arch. Immediately again **TR** up a gravel track which soon becomes grassy. Pass through a metal gate into a field and continue ahead with a wire fence to the left. At the far end go through a wire gate. Shortly pass through a metal gate into another field and slightly **BR** to the **URH** corner to **TR** through a wooden gate into *Ebsbury Copse*. Immediately **TL** along a grassy track and continue ahead across various junctions to a metalled lane. **TR** and, at a crossroads ahead, **TL** along another lane. Shortly **CL** into the long straight lane through Grovely Wood. Eventually, about 1 mile on, after passing several tracks to both sides *(see map)*, sharply **TL** opposite two nursery plantations along a broad clearly-defined gravel track. This quickly descends to **X** the head of a combe and up again. Continue along, then down towards the village below. Just above the line of houses, **TL** along a broad grassy track. At the end **TR** along a lane and under the railway arch to the pub.

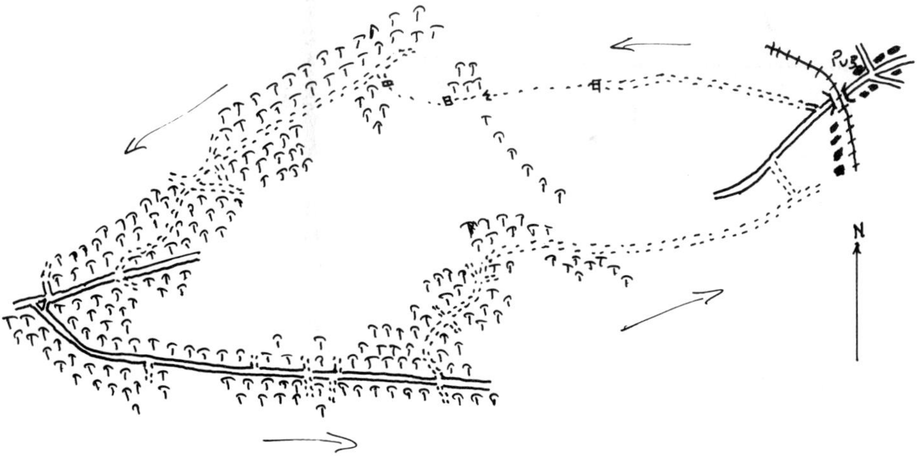

Travellers in the Vale of Pewsey, Honeystreet

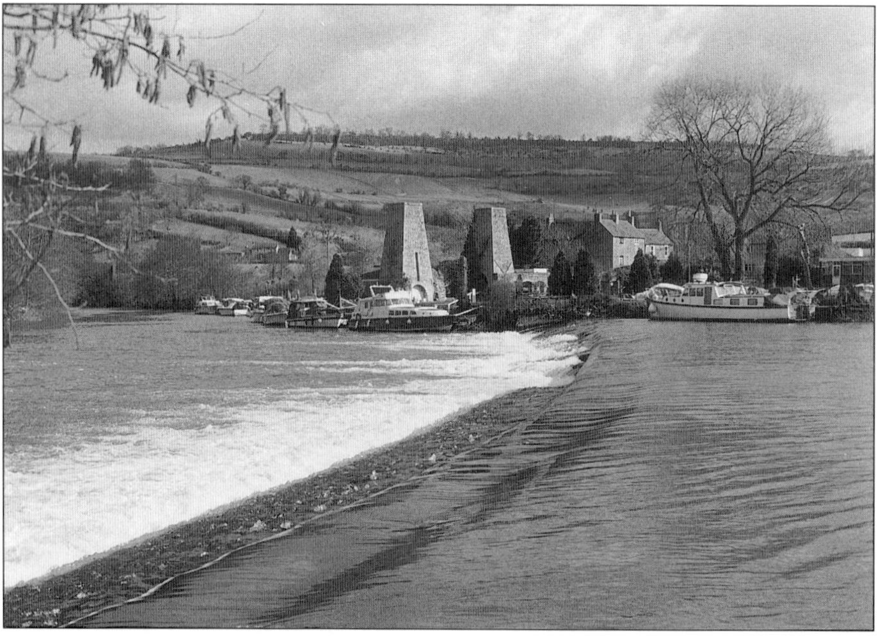

Kelston Hill and Kelston Mills from Saltford Lock

HONEYSTREET **THE BARGE INN**

O.S. MAP NO. 173 : 101 616

From the village of Alton Barnes go south for a half mile, cross a bridge over the Kennet and Avon canal and, immediately, turn right into a timber yard. The inn is at the end of this access lane.
There is plenty of parking space here.

HOURS:	Sunday	12.00 - 3.00	:	7.00 - 10.30
	Weekdays	11.00 - 3.00	:	6.00 - 11.00
	Saturday	11.00	————	11.00

N.B. These are summer hours. No meals on Tuesday evening.

This stone building was erected in 1858 by the proprietor of the timber and boat building company for employees, locals and passing barges. The location was partly determined by the refusal of Alton parish council to the north to allow the erection of ale houses. Nevertheless, standing on the edge of the canal as it does, it is ideal for a warm day, seated outside and overlooking the rolling hills beyond. Originally, it included stables and a shop. Now it has two bars, one being a games room with a seven feet long pool table, and a dining area next to the main bar.

A Courage house — Best and Directors — it is admirably kept by Tony and Janet Molland (a 'darling' lady) who create a warm, friendly and welcoming atmosphere. A life of variety was begun by Tony in variety — the theatrical kind. He was also for twenty years a pilot in the RAF, part of which was served in Borneo, then for a further ten years flew for the Sultan of Oman.

Bar snacks and a continuously changing restaurant menu cater for all tastes and appetites, including vegetarians and children. (Having spent a night on the Molland's narrowboat moored by the inn, I began the day with a substantial and delicious breakfast, so I can personally recommend Janet's cooking).

Children are welcome.
Dogs too.

Set in the Vale of Pewsey outward routes climb and pass along the open chalk downs to make an easy return along the banks of the Kennet and Avon canal. Only the shortest of the walks here does not include Wansdyke, an impressive ditch thought to be a Saxon fortification against the Danes. Yet all pass by on the side of Milk Hill and another of the white horses so characteristic of Wessex. While walking Wansdyke I observed two kestrels hunting down a small hedgerow bird — it was too far to see what variety. It took refuge in the tangled twists and turns of a stunted leafless thornbush, the hawks hovering unable to reach it. Only as I took a step closer were the hunters disturbed. They peeled swiftly away northwards over All Cannings Down.

Walk 1	**4½ miles**	**Parts A B E**
Walk 2	**5½ miles**	**Parts A C D E**
Walk 3	**7 miles**	**Parts A C F**
Walk 4	**7½ miles**	**Parts A C G H**
Walk 5	**8 miles**	**Parts A C G J**

A Return to the road and **TL** over the bridge. Shortly **TR** at a sign to *St Mary's Saxon Church,* then **TL** through a turnstile along a cobbled path. **FR** to **X** 2 bridges. Ahead the path turns right towards the church, but **TL** across the field to a small wooden gate to the left of the building ahead. Exit onto a road. **TR** then, by a phone box, **TL** up a drive and **FR** up a broad grassy track which narrows above before it enters a field with a stile immediately ahead. **X** onto a road and **TR** to pass through the large wooden gate almost opposite. **TL** up the embankment and on round the hill to a broad grass path. This remains generally level along the side of the hill to the White Horse. Pass above the enclosure to **X** a stile by a small wooden gate in a wire fence. Ahead pass between 2 parallel wire fences and **CR** to **X** a stile.

B **TL** down along a wire fence and again **TL** down the edge of a combe to a small wooden gate near the bottom. Here **TL** round the base of the hill, dropping down to **X** a stile onto a broad path between fields. Go ahead away from the hill to a junction of paths. Keeping to the left of a wire fence, continue to the road below and **TR**.

C **BL** to **X** a second stile and **CL** around the top of the combe. **TR** over a third stile and **BL** down to pass through a wooden gate onto a broad gravel track. **TR** and shortly **TL** over a stile onto a path above the dyke.

D Having viewed the dyke, return to the gravel track and **TR** down to a junction. **FL** and again **FL** of a barn towards another barn, then **BR** beside the farm track to the road ahead.

E Carefully **X** the road to go along the lane through *Stanton St Bernard.* **CR** round to another lane, then **TL** to the canal beyond the village. **X** the bridge and **TL** along the far bank to the inn.

F Having viewed the dyke, return to the gravel track and **TR** down to a junction. **FR** down to a metal gate and go through onto the road at a T-junction. Go straight ahead to the canal bridge and **TL** to the inn.

G Go along the dyke to **X** a stile by a gate and on to a junction beyond.

H At the junction **TL** along a wire fence over the crest of *Tan Hill.* **X** a stile by a wooden gate and **BL** down to **X** a wooden fence near a metal gate. Here either (a) **BL** up to and over the ancient earthworks to **FR** over *Clifford's Hill,* then **CR** along the crest; or (b) continue down the path round the base of the hill. Both paths merge by a stile and metal gate, the road directly below. Carefully **X** the road to the farmyard and go through the wooden gate into a field. **X** to the right hand corner and over a stile into the next field. Keeping close to the hedge on the right, go on to the canal ahead, marked by an iron lozenge. **X** the bridge and **TL** to the inn.

J At the junction **X** the stile by the wooden gate and **TL**. Shortly **TL** through a metal gate onto a metalled track and down to a final metal gate onto a road. **TR** along the road and shortly **TL** along a lane. At the end go straight on along a bridleway to **X** the canal. **TL** for the inn.

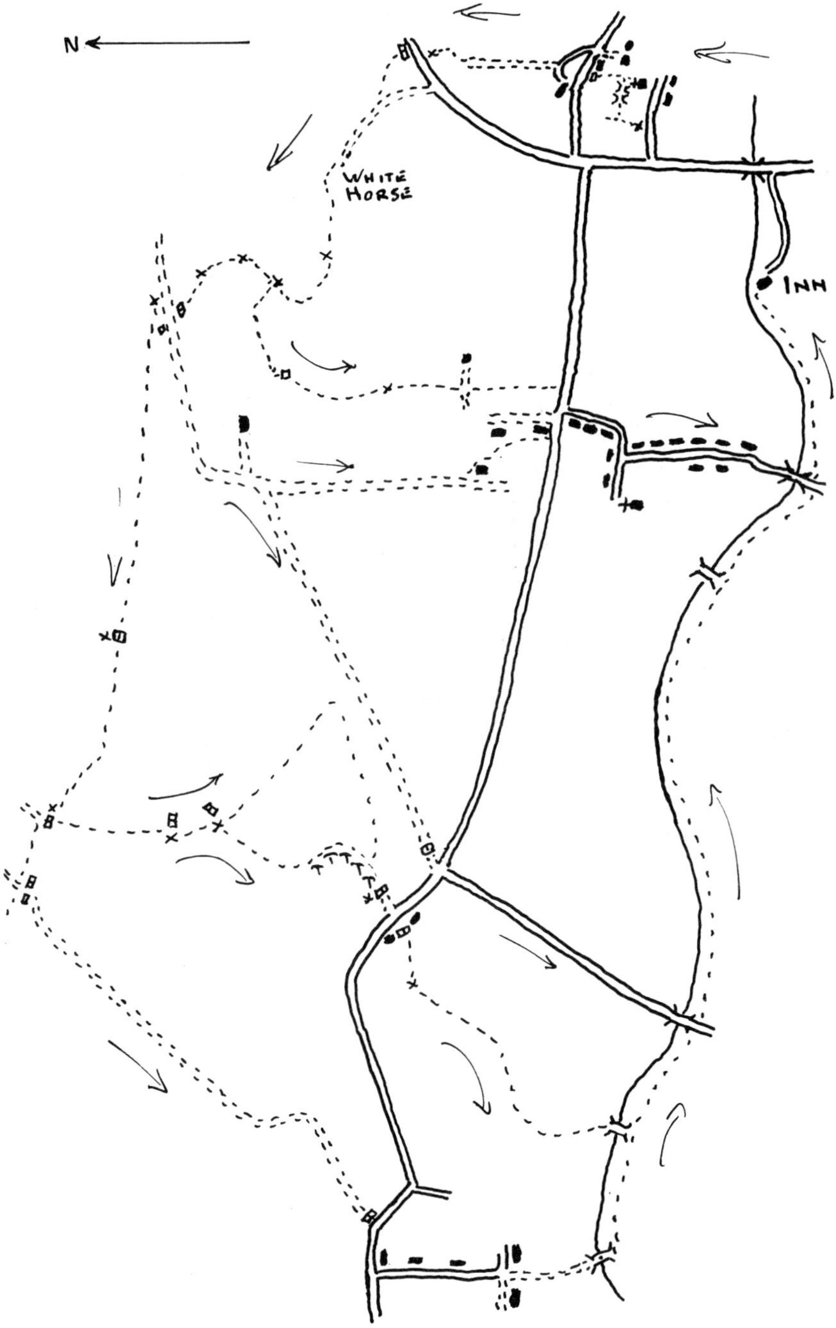
N
WHITE
HORSE
INN

O.S. MAP NO. 183 : 810 417

At Longbridge Deverill, on the A350 south of Warminster, take the road towards Maiden Bradley. About two miles on, turn right to Horningsham where the pub is situated by the central crossroads.
Parking space for about a dozen cars is provided in the car park, otherwise park on the nearby roads.

HOURS:	Sunday	12.00 - 2.30	:	7.00 - 10.30
	Weekdays	11.00 - 2.30	:	6.00 - 11.00
	Saturday	11.00 - 2.30	:	6.00 - 11.00

This dignified stone building, set square on the village crossroads, has been licensed for over two hundred years. Joe and Beryl Lovatt, in the licensed trade for thirty-five years, have extended the sense of dignity to the interior: the lounge and restaurant are fine rooms. Vegetarian and children's meals are available on the full and varied menu, and a variety of bar snacks should satisfy those short on appetite or time. There is also a public bar, skittle alley and beer garden.

Joe's well-kept Wadworth's 6X, Bass, Eldridge Pope's Best and Dorchester Bitters are complemented by Hacker Pschorr Export lager, with Wilkins' Farmhouse cider in summer.

Unfortunately, children are not allowed inside.
On the other hand dogs, having no legal constraint, are.

HORNINGSHAM — THE BATH ARMS

These walks pass over part of Longleat's parkland, pasture and arable land, through coniferous and mixed woodland. There are lakes and at least three hills together offering views to the south and round to the north-west. From Heaven's Gate above the park you can see beyond Frome round to the Mendips and across towards Wincanton with Longleat house supine below. Yet I prefer the more open, detailed scene from Brimsdown: to the south White Sheet Hill (Kilmington, page 57) with Shaftesbury and Duncliffe Hill beyond, across to the south-west Little Knoll and Long Knoll with Alfred's Tower behind (Stourton, page 83), while the Mendips and Frome are again visible.

Walk 1	**2½ miles**	**Parts A B**
Walk 2	**6 miles**	**Parts A C D**
Walk 3	**7 miles**	**Parts A C E**

A **TL** down the lane into *Longleat*. Past the gatehouse **BR** to pass between lakes, and **X** a stile. **TR** uphill through the oaks to **X** another stile in a wire fence ahead. **TR** again up to *Heaven's Gate*. At the top **BR** through a small wooden gate next to a large wooden gate and shortly **TR** downhill. Pass a cottage to go through another small wooden gate next to a large one, and on down the lane.

B Go down to the road just beyond the church, **TR** and **FR** back to the inn.

C **TL** at a crossroads, following the lane down to a road. **TR** and immediately **L** up another road. Shortly **TR** along a track, **X** another road to go up another track to pass through a large wooden gate into a field. Go up to another wooden gate, through a spinney and into the wood ahead. *(This is Bidcombe Hill)*. Exit through a large metal gate to **TR** onto another track and immediately through a wire gate. **BL** to **X** a wooden fence, then slightly **BR** to the far rim of *Brimsdown Hill*, keeping a copse of beeches to the right and pass through a small wooden gate. Go on to the bottom and **TR** to **X** a stile into a field. Make way to the metal gate on the far side and, similarly, in the next field to the metal gate right of the farmhouse ahead. Exit onto a road and **TL**.

D Pass the farmhouse to **TR** opposite the first barn through a metal gate. **CR** down the combe, through a metal gate and shortly over a stile by a metal gate to pass along the **RH** edge of a copse and through another metal gate onto a lane. **TL**, following the lane round to a road. **TL** to the inn.

E Follow the road to a junction. **TR** up to where the road turns right. **BL** through a large wooden gate and down the woodland track to the bottom. Exit onto another road. Go straight on and round to the inn.

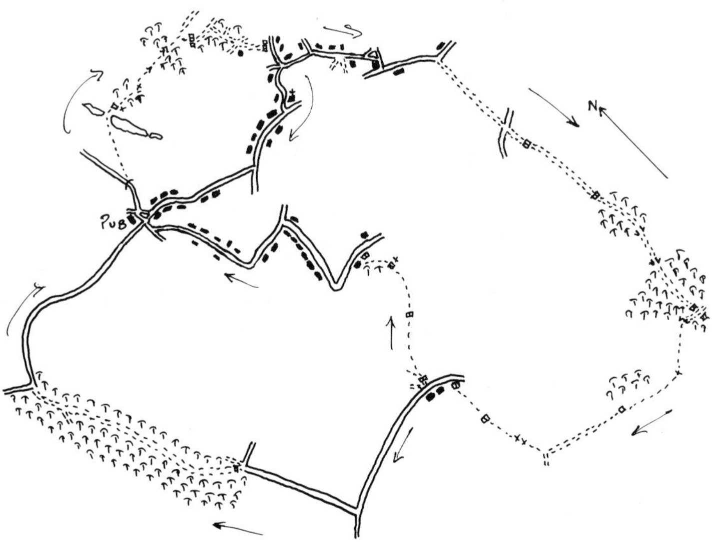

O.S. MAP NO. 173 : 038 633

Take the A361 from Devizes towards Swindon and, just over a mile from the town centre, turn right to Horton. The inn is by the bridge over the canal.
There is parking on site and a lay-by opposite.

HOURS:	Sunday	12.00 - 3.00	:	7.00 - 10.30
	Weekdays	12.00 - 2.30	:	6.30 - 11.00
	Saturday	12.00 - 2.30	:	6.30 - 11.00

Attractively situated alongside the Kennet and Avon canal with views of the surrounding hills, the garden is a good place to be on a warm day. Previously, this brick and slate building was a terrace of two houses and a bakery and mill, becoming a pub in 1810. With the construction of the canal the road had to be raised to pass over the bridge. Consequently, the old ground floor is now below ground level and a new top storey had to be added to retain the original height. Anthony and Jill Adamson have created a homely, unpretentious air in the two bar areas — a pool room is adjacent. Anthony is well versed in local history, has been connected with the restoration of the canal, and hires boats from here.

Being a Wadworth's house, 6X and IPA are kept. Food is limited to filled rolls and ploughman's, but hot meals may be provided by prior arrangement.

The pool room is open to families.
Dogs are probably acceptable, but check first with Anthony.

North-west of Horton is Roundway Hill and Roundway Down where in 1643 the Royalists secured a heavy defeat of the Roundheads. The outward route beyond Bishops Cannings passes close by here before ascending to the Wansdyke, the impressive defensive earthwork probably erected by the West Saxons to keep the Danes at bay. All walks begin and end along part of the Kennet and Avon canal where it loops around the village of Horton.

Walk 1	**5½ miles**	**Parts A B**
Walk 2	**6½ miles**	**Parts A C**
Walk 3	**7½ miles**	**Parts A D**

A **TR** over the bridge, then **TL** along the towpath. **TL** over the swing bridge, **X** a stile by a metal gate and **FL** along a metal track to *Bishops Cannings*. Beyond the first houses **TL** along *Church Walk*, go through the churchyard, and **TL** again along the road. **TR** opposite a pub along a gravelled track to **X** a stile by a metal gate into a field. Go ahead to **X** a stile in a wire fence into the next field. Make way to a stile to the left of the farm opposite. **X** into the farmyard and **TR** between sheds to a road. **TL** up to a main road and carefully go over to **X** a stile in a wire fence onto a track and **TR.** Where the track curves steeply uphill **TR** through a small wooden gate. Go through a narrow copse, briefly along the edge of a field and down a track to a road. **TL**, then carefully **X** over to **FR** along a path through the farm almost opposite. At a junction **TR** up to a pair of stiles either side of the track. **TR** over a stile above the *Wansdyke*. Ahead **X** a stile into the main road. Through the drive opposite **BR** to **X** a stile back onto the dyke. Ahead pass on to a track between a pair of stiles.

B Here **TR** down the track into the hamlet of *Bourton*. **FR** along a lane, past barns, then **TL** to a triple fork. **FR** round to **X** a stile next to a white thatched cottage and **BL** across a field on a grass path to **X** a bridge ahead. **BL** to the swing bridge on the canal and **TR** to the inn.

C Continue on over a stile to a second track between a pair of stiles. Here **TR** and pass a barn to a junction by a farm below. **X** the stile in the wire fence opposite, then **BL** to **X** another stile in the far corner. Go ahead over 2 more stiles beyond. Ahead a fifth stile leads over a bridge into the next field. **TR** along the perimeter to a white thatched cottage and a stile in a paddock fence on the right, but sharply **TL** across the field on a grass path to **X** a bridge ahead. **BL** to the swing bridge on the canal and **TR** to the inn.

D Continue on over a stile to a second track between a pair of stiles, then on to a third track. **TR** along the grassy path, keeping a wire fence to the right. Go on over the crest of *Easton Hill*, through a metal gate and down to the road below. **TR** to the canal. **X** the bridge and **TR** along the towpath back to the inn.

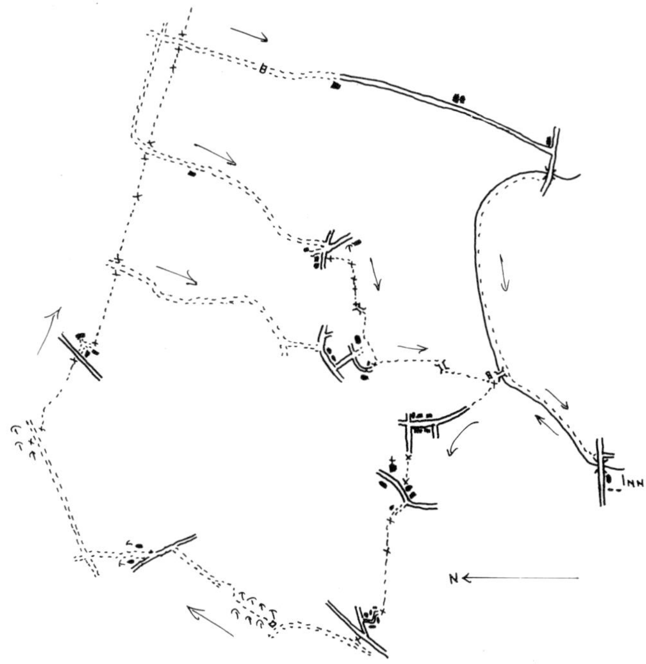

O.S. MAP NO. 183 : 787 354

The inn stands on its own midway between Maiden Bradley and Mere on the B3092. The car park and two lay-bys together provide about forty spaces.

HOURS:	Sunday	12.00 - 3.00	:	7.00 - 10.30
	Weekdays	11.00 - 3.00	:	6.30 - 11.00
	Saturday	11.00 - 3.00	:	6.30 - 11.00

N.B. No food served Monday and Tuesday evenings.

The Red Lion Inn owes its origins to an early seventeenth century farmhouse. This was later converted by the landowner to a pub for estate workers. Eventually, it became a drovers' inn and post-house for the coach route up Whitesheet Hill to Salisbury, for which purpose two horses were kept to add to the regular team of four. Such history seems to linger in the stone-flagged floor, beamed ceiling and open fireplaces — a settle by the larger fire — of the bar. Though the horses have gone, Lady, the black Labrador, supplies a welcome. Do not the dominoes, cribbage and shove-halfpenny boards also reflect that period?

The house has been ably and enthusiastically run by Chris Gibbs since 1978. He regularly serves Butcombe Bitter and Bass, to which is added a list of frequently changing guest beers (I had an Old Hookey last time) and a draught cider — currently Stonehouse Inch's Dry. While there is no restaurant service, there may be up to seven home-made plated hot dishes, including vegetarian, and the bar snacks are excellent (the home-cooked ham in my sandwich was the best I have had in a long while and attractively served with crisp side salad).

Unfortunately, it is not possible to take children inside, though there is a large garden overlooking Whitesheet Hill.
Dogs may, naturally, join Lady at the bar.

KILMINGTON — THE RED LION

Whitesheet Hill at a little over 800 feet lies on the western edge of the chalklands. With characteristically steep sides and gently-rounded top, it is invaded from the north-east by a beautiful deep combe. To the west are the Mendip Hills, north is Brimsdown Hill (Horningsham, page 53), while to the south another deep combe leads the eye across the town of Mere towards Dorset. A National Trust property and nature reserve, it is possible to wander within the boundary and to inspect tumuli and earthworks. It is also the sight of other recreational activities. Radio-controlled model aircraft are flown and I have seen a hunt galloping across the combe and up Rodmead Hill opposite.

Walk 1	**3½ miles**	**Parts A B**
Walk 2	**4½ miles**	**Parts A C**

A **TR** along the road for about 400 yards and **FR** along a track just before a farm. Eventually **BR** onto a lane by *Elm Farm*. Ahead the lane turns right.

B Here **TR** with the lane to pass through double metal gates, then shortly **TR** through a wooden gate. **BL** directly up *Whitesheet Hill*. On the far side of the down a number of gates lead onto a broad rutted track traversing the crest. Exit through any one of these and **TR** down the track, which eventually becomes a lane, back to the pub.

C Here go ahead through a metal gate into a field. Keeping close to the hedge on the left, continue to wooden gate ahead. Pass through into the next field and, still keeping close to the hedge on the left, exit through a gap in the far hedge onto a lane. **TR**, pass a farm, and, shortly after the lane becomes a gently rising track, approach a metal gate at the base of *Rodmead Hill*. Do not go through but **TR** through a gap in the hedge and continue along the broad chalk track curving around the base of the hill. Pass through a copse to the hilltop and, as the track turns left, **TR** through a small wooden gate in a wire fence. *(Enjoy the view back towards Long Knoll and Little Knoll)*. Continue along the crest of the hill, a wire fence to the right. Go on to pass through a metal gate in a wire fence onto a broad stony track. *(For the view down the southern combe, Great Bottom, go through the gate opposite. Observing the warning signs, go ahead as far as you wish and return)*. **TR** along the track, which eventually drops down and becomes a lane, back to the pub.

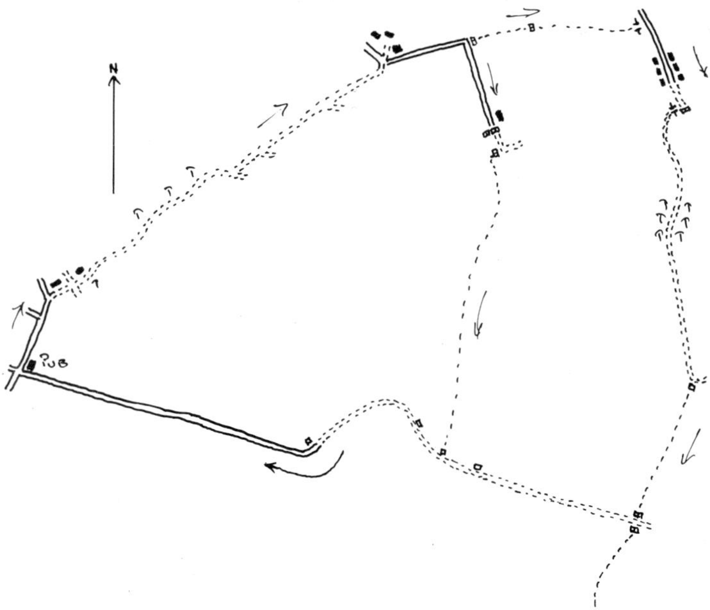

O.S. MAP NO. 184 : 956 265

From the west, go through Ludgershall on the A432 and, on the eastern outskirts, turn left. Follow the road for about two miles, past a T-junction, to the next junction in the village itself. The inn is opposite.
Ample parking is provided in the car park.

HOURS:	Sunday	12.00 - 3.00	:	7.00 - 10.30
	Weekdays	11.00 - 3.00	:	6.00 - 11.30
	Saturday	11.00 - 3.00	:	6.00 - 11.30

A very attractive three hundred year old thatched inn is efficiently run by Mr and Mrs Simmonds. Water-colour paintings decorate the single bar and dining-room. Vegetarian dishes appear on the daily-changing menu, although children's meals do not. An example of what the chef has offered is as follows: frogs' legs or garlic snails or rollmops in madeira; braised chicken in brandy sauce or red snapper creole or grilled turbot in lemon butter; cider syllabub or crepes suzettes or bread and butter pudding. Choose real ales from Bass, Wadworth's 6X, Adnam's Bitter, Ballard's Best, and John Smith's Bitter.

Children may come into the dining-room.
Dogs may be brought in only on a lead.

LOWER CHUTE — THE HATCHET INN

The two walks here include a part of the unusual Chute Causeway, a circular roadway, mostly on a ridge, around a triangle of hills. The longer route will take you up the 846 feet Haydown Hill. On top is an ancient fortification, while in the combe below is a shooting school — violent activities for such a beautiful and, when the shotguns are broken, peaceful area. Is it my imagination or are there fewer pheasants hereabouts? I spoke to two gamekeepers who certainly appeared plump and healthy. Their ancestors were not so lucky. In 1665 villagers from nearby Vernham Dean who had contact with the plague were persuaded by their rector to isolate themselves on Haydown Hill. In fear he failed to fulfil his promise of regular supplies. Those who did not die of the disease starved. Doubly ironical the village was nevertheless ravaged and the rector himself become a victim.

Walk 1	**5 miles**	**Parts A B D**
Walk 2	**6½ miles**	**Parts A C D**

A **TL** from the inn, then **L** again at the village cross. Go up the lane, past 2 lanes to the left and **TL** again along a third lane which shortly becomes a track. **FL** along the edge of a wood to a metal gate and stile. **X** into a field and go up to a stile to the left of a large copse ahead. **X** over and **BR** up to a point about 50 yards to the right of a corrugated barn ahead. Here **X** a stile in a wire fence and continue on to **X** another stile in a wire fence. Continue to a metal gate and stile and **X** on to a road. Go along the road, then down past a right fork to **TL** over a stile into a field. **BL** down to another in the **LLH** corner and **X** onto a lane.

B **TL** along the lane to a farm ahead and an uphill track on the left.

C **TR** along the lane for about ½ mile, then **TL** up a track and past a house to the treeline above. **TL** and **X** a stile. Continue towards the hilltop, roughly parallel with the treeline, to **TR** near the end of the wood and **X** a stile into a broad field on the hilltop. **X** to the triangulation point, then **BR** down to pass through a gap in the wire fence ahead. **BL** to the far corner, go through a wire gate onto a track and immediately through a metal gate. Immediately **TL** down a grass track to the base of the hill, **X** a stile and go into a farm. Ahead is an uphill track.

D Follow this track up to the ridge, over the road, and down to a T-junction. **TR**, then shortly **TL** to a lane and onto a road. Go straight on round to the inn.

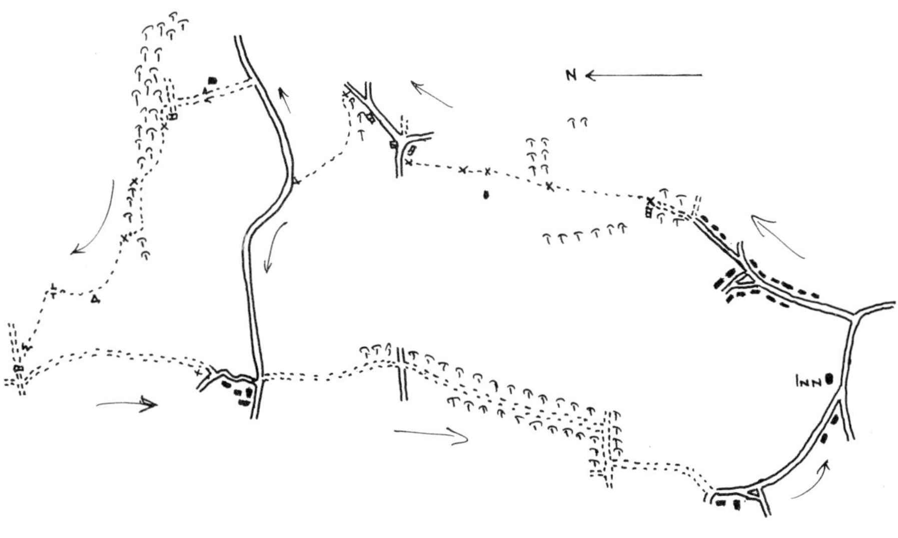

O.S. MAP NO. 173 : 934 869

Located in town, almost at the bottom of High Street.
Park in High Street or above in Cross Hayes.

For myself The Smoking Dog has many points of interest and has become a personal favourite. Not only is this the sole town-located pub in this publication, but the discerning toper will find a greater variety of real ales than at other hostelries herein. Five regulars (Usher's Best, Smiles' Best, Wiltshire's Stonehenge Best, Bunce's Old Smokey, Theakston's Old Peculier) are supported by numerous guest beers. On one occasion I was forced to choose from those five and Banks and Taylor's Shefford Old Dark (SOD), Premier Ale's Maiden's Ruin and Wiltshire's Stonehenge Exhibition Ale.

The food is good. I can personally recommend the game soup, thankfully served not only with warm bread but with a generous portion of butter in a ramekin. At the time cassoulet and pork tenderloin were also on the blackboard with its daily-changing fare.

The Cotswold stone, plaster and beamed interior delivers a bright airiness to the bar. A dining area is separated to the rear and, useful in summer, out back is a small pleasant garden overlooking rooftops.

Just as I had concluded that The Smoking Dog had the feeling of a young person's pub, three smartly-dressed and well-spoken pensioners entered and ordered the strongest ale in the house.

A pleasant rather than outstanding walk which runs along part of the old town wall and the bank of the Avon at three different points, takes in views of the abbey and, for contrast, passes by a sewage works. Nothing difficult.

Walk 4 miles

TL, **X** the road and **TR** down *Kingswall* which soon becomes a path. **FL** down to *Burnivale* and sharply **TL** down a narrow path towards a field beyond. **TR** across 2 bridges and **R** again along the bank. *(Look out for dabchicks, moorhens and wagtails).* **X** the stone stile and sharply **TL** up a metalled track. At the top **TR** through a wooden gate just before a farmhouse. **X** a field towards a tall house. Just before it and to the left in a narrow gap in the hedge is a small wooden fence. Go over onto a stony track and **TL**. Ahead, go through a metal gate towards a farmyard. Pass through 3 more metal gates. At a triple junction continue ahead through the **LH** metal gate. Pass between a clump of trees and a derelict building. Beyond **BL** towards a wooden gate in the hedge ahead. Go through and along to a road. **TL** along the pavement for about 100 yards and look for a small gap in the stone wall opposite, just before the first house on the right. Carefully **X** the road, go through the gap and over a stile into a field. **BR** to the middle of the **RH** hedge to go through a metal gate. **BL** up to a metal gate in the **URH** corner. Go through and on up the hill. Again, go through a metal gate in the **ULH** corner. Slightly **BL** down to a small gap in the hedge below. Go through and over the wooden fence. **BR** across to the river bank and bridge. **TR** over the bridge, past factory gates and a metal gate on the left.

TL the second metal gate. Pass to the **R** of a line of trees and go up to a wooden gate ahead. Go through and **TR** along the hedge, pass through a metal gate, then drop down to another metal gate. Go through, over the bridge, and immediately **TL** through a metal gate into a field. Sharply **TR** up to a wooden fence. Go over into the next field and, keeping close to the hedge on the left, drop down to 2 metal gates. *(Notice the abbey ahead).* Go through the one between 2 wire fences and pass the sewage works. *(Notice the lack of view).* Exit onto a driveway and follow it round, along the river and under a flyover. Now **CL** along a lane, *Baskerville*, that passes the bowls club, crosses a hump bridge over the *River Ingleburn*, finally joining *High Street*. **TR** up to a well-earned drink.

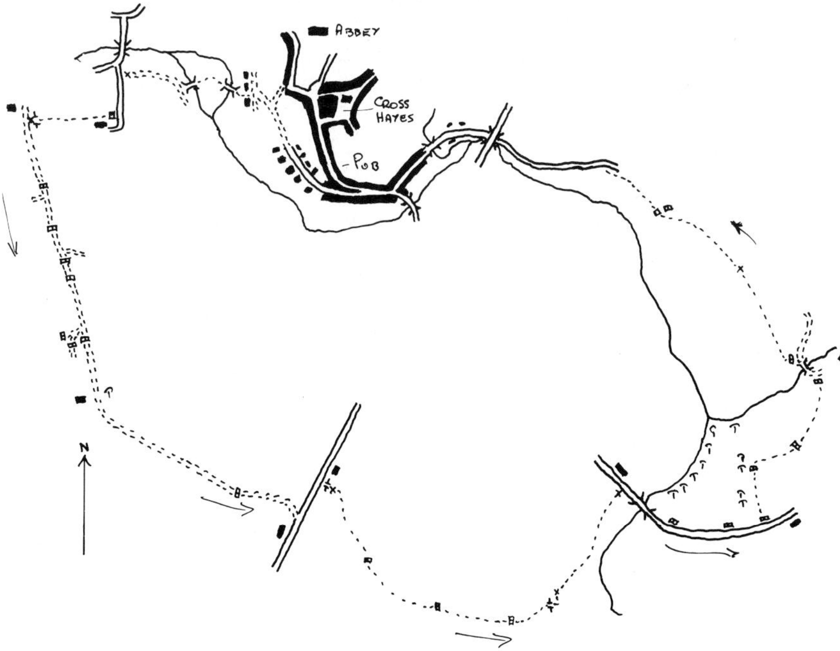

O.S. MAP NO. 184 (also 195) : 254 174

Take the A36 south-east from Salisbury and, about nine miles on, turn right towards Landford and Bramshaw. After about another mile and a half turn right again at a cross roads to Nomansland and the inn on the green.
Park outside or along the green opposite.

HOURS:	Sunday	12.00 - 3.00	:	7.00 - 10.30
	Weekdays	11.00 - 3.00	:	6.00 - 11.00
	Saturday	11.00	———	11.00

N.B. No food Sunday and Monday evenings.

This early nineteenth century Whitbread pub is run by ex-rock-n-roll drummer Stan Poole and his wife, Ruth. Those of you who remember them might like to ask him about Dave Dee, Dozy, Beaky, Mick and Tich. Also of some interest is the fact that the building stands on the very edge of Wiltshire, the front steps are in Hampshire. So sit in Wiltshire and enjoy the cricket in Hampshire on the green opposite.

The single L-shaped bar has a thatched ceiling, half-timbered walls and log fires. Apart from a selection of bar snacks there is a home-cooked 'special' most days. You may wash this down with a Strong Country Bitter or Marston's Pedigree.

No children are allowed in.
Dogs are.

Here are woods and the heathered, sandy heathland of the New Forest; a large pond with ducks, geese and swans; wild ponies graze with pigs and cattle; and deer and hawks may be seen. Look carefully and you may also discover a second pub — The Royal Oak at Fritham. Try varying the combination of routes.

NOMANSLAND — THE LAMB INN

Walk 1	**5 miles**	**Parts A C D F**
Walk 2	**5½ miles**	**Parts A C E F**
Walk 3	**5½ miles**	**Parts B C D F**
Walk 4	**6½ miles**	**Parts B C E F**

TR from the inn. **TL** along a broad track opposite the garage.

A Almost immediately **TR** and **BL** along a grassy path. **X** another broad track and continue uphill. Soon **BR** uphill and, on meeting a track from the left, **TR**. Pass up through a delightful group of beeches and out to *Pipers Wait* parking-picnic area. Slightly **BL** along a broad path towards a line of trees ahead. Shortly the path joins a broad bridleway. Aim for the **RH** end of this line.

B **X** a culvert and **TR** down another track to **X** a stream and **FL** gently uphill. **X** 2 more small bridges and **FR** after the second. Pass 2 wooden posts on the right and **BR** up a steeper path. **X** over a thick, fallen tree trunk and pass between 2 more wooden posts. Continue climbing steeply until the path breaks out at the top. Go on to **X** a broad stony track and **CL** along another path to the right of a line of trees.

C Beyond the line of trees **FR** along a broad path to a road junction. Carefully **X** to the *Fritham* road. On the **RH** verge take a path almost parallel to the road and continue ahead as the road curves left. About a mile ahead the level path enters a line of trees. Keeping a wire fence and pasture to the left, continue to *The Royal Oak*. After further refreshment **TR** down the lane to *Eyeworth Pond*. **TR** into the car park. Having fed the ducks, follow the broad stony track at the far end into the wood.

D Follow this track up to the road. **BL** across the road and down the track to merge with a path from the left along a wire fence.

E Emerging from the wood, **BL** along a narrow grassy path and over a stream. Climb up towards a copse to the right of a thicker wood. Pass through and slightly **BL**. Continue uphill, the woods still to the left. As the path levels out it joins another from the left. **BR**, passing through the **LH** side of another thicker copse ahead. **X** the road ahead and continue to the wire fence ahead. **TR** along the path, following the fence down to the bottom to merge with another path from the right.

F Climb up to the road and continue down the road to the inn.

O.S. MAP NO. 174 (also 173) : 203 743

The pub is located close to the flyover taking the A345 Marlborough-Swindon road over a minor road to the village. Access is via a feeder road from the A345 south of the village. Parking for about 25 cars is provided and there are no restrictions in the village.

HOURS:	Sunday	12.00 - 3.00	:	7.00 - 10.30
	Weekdays	12.00 - 2.00	:	6.30 - 11.00
	Saturday	11.00 - 2.30	:	6.00 - 11.00

The Old Crown is ably and stimulatingly run by Brian Dean and Christopher Cannon. Stimulatingly, because Brian invites patrons to "come along for your helping of warm, friendly abuse". If he has as much success as the famed landlord of 'The Spread Eagle' at Thame sixty years ago, The Old Crown may become an even more popular pub. The attractive restaurant is immaculate, while the single bar of brick and stone has a fine oval mirror in a gilt surround and a Victorian copy of the Admiral's Cup.

For real ale drinkers the hosts keep Wadworth's 6X and two guest beers. Bar snacks are served, but the restaurant menu is the house speciality. There could be crevettes or frogs' legs to begin; breast of duck with onion, cherry, cider and orange sauce or halibut in shallot sauce; and chocolate roulade or black cherries in hot brandy and cream to finish. Vegetarians are not overlooked and children's meals are available on request.

Children are allowed in the restaurant.
Dogs may be brought in at the management's discretion.

OGBOURNE ST GEORGE — THE OLD CROWN

An historic walk over chalk downs and part of the Ridgeway path. The route follows Smeathe's Ridge up to Barbury Castle, an Iron Age hillfort which gives its name to the battle fought nearby in AD 566 and which helped establish the kingdom of Wessex. Return either below the ridge or, the longer way, back across the downs on the old coaching route between Salisbury and Swindon by the racehorse gallops and Ogbourne St Andrew.

On the ridge are ancient burial mounds known as bowl barrows, while below is a more unusual disc barrow associated with the burial of women. Just below the castle and the car-park are ancient field systems.

Walk 1	**7½ miles**	**Parts A B**
Walk 2	**9½ miles**	**Parts A C**

A **TL** and immediately **TR** at the T-junction. Go through the village and, shortly after the road turns sharply right, **TL** up a broad track. Ahead **X** a stile by a metal gate, and go on through a second metal gate to pass through a small wooden gate by a metal gate onto a broad track about 2 miles from the stile. *(This is Smeathe's Ridge).* **TR** and pass a farm, where the track becomes a metalled lane, then **TL** through a small wooden gate to pass the car park and on to the fort.

B Return through the car-park to the lane and **TL** downhill. Shortly **TR** and **X** a stile by a metal gate. Go down to a junction and **FR** round the base of the ridge, below a copse, to **TR** just after the track swings left to the farm below. Go down to the road and **X** into the field opposite. **BL** down to pass between a spinney to the left and a paddock to the right. *(A stile is to be placed in the wire fence here).* **CR** round behind the church down to the first of 3 stiles leading up to the houses ahead. After the third, go through a gap in the fence and **CR** between houses to the road. **TL** for the pub.

C Go back to the farm and follow the broad track over the downs for about 2 miles. Where a wire fence to the left ends **FL** towards a barn. Before it **TL** over a stile by a metal gate and go down to **X** another stile by a metal gate. Pass a barn and shortly **TR** onto a farm drive and along to *Ogbourne St Andrew.* Past the church **TL** and, as the lane swings right, go ahead along a broad track to **TR** at a junction about 1 mile on. Soon **TL** over a stile by a metal gate immediately before a farm and follow the paddock fence past a wind pump. **X** another stile into the adjacent field and **BR** down to **X** a pair of stiles and footbridge. **BL** along a wire fence to **X** a stile, the next field, and a final stile into a narrow passage to the road. **TR** for the pub.

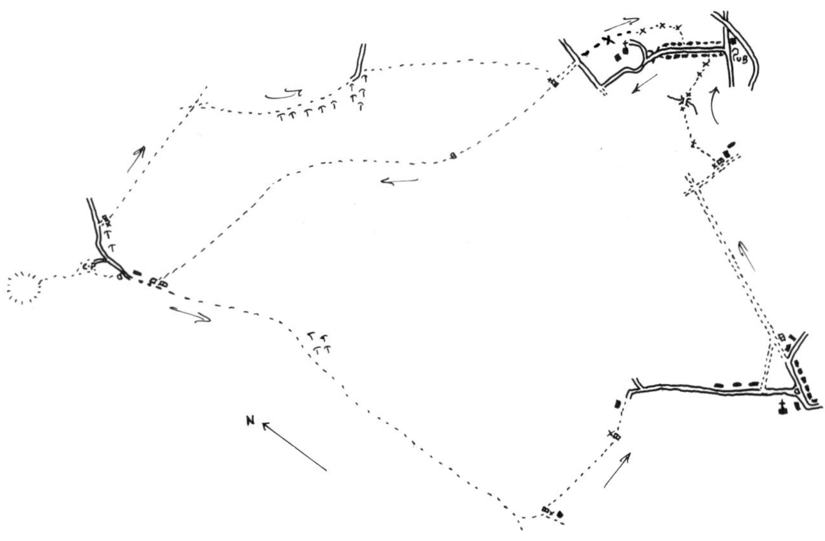

O.S. MAP NO. 172 : 744 734

The Swan Inn is on the A46, just north of the junction with the A420 east of Bristol. There are two car parks for about thirty cars.

HOURS:	Sunday	12.00 - 3.00	:	7.00 - 10.30
	Weekdays	11.00 - 2.30	:	6.00 - 11.00
	Saturday	11.00 - 2.30	:	6.00 - 11.00

N.B. Main meals are not served until 7.00

Once a terrace of three miners' cottages the building dates back to the early eighteenth century. It has a single bar with stone-clad walls, beamed ceiling and a large open fireplace. The pub and its hosts, David and Shirley Watton, have close links with the state of Pennsylvania in USA (David had just returned from a visit when I arrived and is currently researching any connection between this hamlet and William Penn) and this is reflected in the memorabilia on show. A large collection of foreign coins is also displayed on the walls.

This is very much a welcoming, friendly house with many regulars. Clearly they like Bass, Archer's Village Bitter, Smiles' Brewery Bitter, Gibbs Mew Salisbury Best, and a different guest beer each week. Bar snacks and main meals may be taken in the dining area, although neither vegetarians nor children are specially catered for.

Children may enter the dining area.
Dogs may come in only at the hosts' discretion — the old problem when serving food.

High Cotswold country and the steep-sided upper combes above Bath are the location for a bracing walk that helps to belie the name of Cold Ashton through which it passes. A shorter walk avoids many of the ups-and-downs yet has some fine aspects.

Walk 1	**2 miles**	**Parts A B D**
Walk 2	**6 miles**	**Parts A C D**

A Carefully **X** the road and **TR** to **X** a stile into a field just beyond the last buildings. Go ahead to pass through a small wooden gate in the far hedge into the next field. Continue through a gap in the far hedge and **TR** to **X** a small bridge across a stream into the adjacent field. **BR** up to pass through a metal gate by the pub above. Carefully **X** the road to go along a gravel track almost opposite. Go on along a path past the church onto another road. **TL** to a double metal gate beyond the last cottage. Here **TR** along the signed path down to and over a stile by a metal gate, then on to a wooden gate. Pass through and down the steep broad track between fields to a large wooden gate ahead with a small one on the right.

B **TR** through the small gate and **CR** around the shoulder of the hill to **BL** past another small wooden gate and along a wire fence to a stile ahead.

C Go through the large gate and follow the broad track down to **CL** around the shoulder of the hill. Where the valley and the stream to the right veer sharply to the left, **X** over to go straight on up the combe ahead on a narrower path. **X** a double stile by a small wooden gate, another stile by a broken stone wall until, almost at the head of the combe, a wire fence impedes further progress. Here **TR** up to **X** a stone stile in the hedge above onto a track enclosed in a double hedge. **TR** to a lane ahead. **TL** and shortly **TR** on another track which soon narrows. **TR** through a metal gate and continue along a hilltop path across a field, a combe to the left. Go through a wooden gate into the next field. Keeping close to the right hand hedge, **TR** through a gap in this hedge and immediately **TL**, the hedge now on the left. Go down to pass through a wire gate and on to a track. **CR** at the farm onto a lane and **TL**. Just past the house below, immediately **TR** to cross a stile between metal gates. **BL** to pass through a wooden gate onto a lane above. **TR** and go on down a broad grassy track. **X** a stile by a metal gate and go through 3 further metal gates. **TR** down to and through a small wooden gate, then **BL** along the stream. **X** the stream to a stile in a wire fence above.

D **X** the stile and go up to pass through a metal gate on the left of houses above. Exit onto a road and **TL**. Pass a T-junction and, just beyond a phone box, **TR** over a stile by a metal gate. **TR** along and round a wall to exit onto a road. Carefully **X** the road, **TL** and immediately **TR** through a gap in the hedge into a field. Make way to a yellow post opposite and **X** a stone stile to diagonally **X** the next field to the inn beyond.

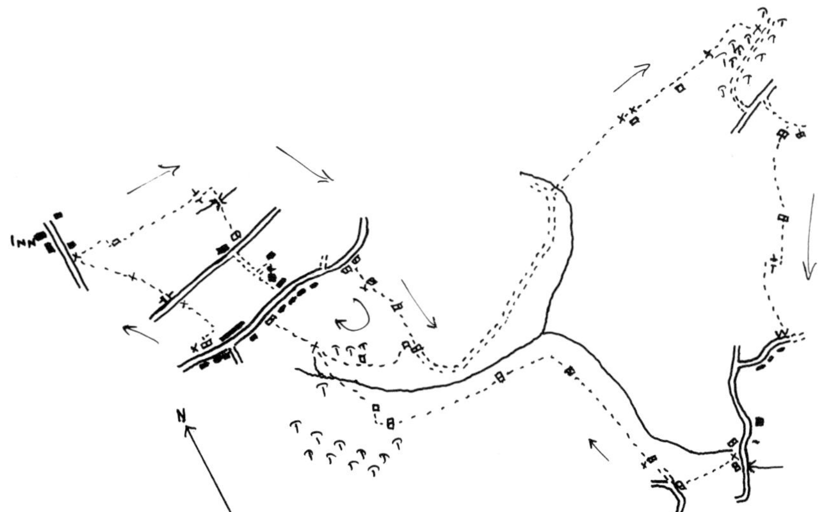

PITTON **THE SILVER PLOUGH**

O.S. MAP NO. 184 : 213 313

From the A30, turn right about three miles east of Salisbury. Pitton is about two miles on and the pub is beyond the crossroads on the far side of the village.
There should be no problem in this ample car park.

HOURS:	Sunday	12.00 - 3.00	:	7.00 - 10.30
	Weekdays	11.00 - 3.00	:	6.00 - 11.00
	Saturday	11.00 - 3.00	:	6.00 - 11.00

N.B. No restaurant service Sunday and Monday evenings, though snacks and blackboard 'specials' are available any evening.

In its time the pub has been a farmhouse, a smithy and a wheelwright's with one corner shop selling local beer and country wines. The ceiling beams were originally part of sailing ships before they came ashore to be used, eventually, in the conversion of the farm to The Silver Plough. From them hang relics of craftsmen's artifacts and a large collection of glass rolling-pins. Today it is under the aegis of a triple partnership — Michael Beckett, Paul Parnell and Charles Manktelow — all experienced in the hotel and catering trade.

There are two bars, serving Wadworth's 6X, John Smith's Bitter, Courage Best and Directors. Yet it is not surprising given the past experience of the partnership, that good food is important here. An à la carte menu is changed monthly and, in addition, a blackboard of four or five 'specials' changes daily. Two main courses may stand as an example: sauté of calves' liver with onions, parsley and cream; medallions of monkfish glazed in mustard and herbs. And as a 'simple' bar snack Wiltshire ham and mushroom tortellini? There should be no problem for vegetarians and there is a limited selection of children's meals.

Hungry children are welcome.
Dogs are not.

PITTON — THE SILVER PLOUGH

From the village the walks follow part of the Clarendon Way — a 30 mile Roman route between Salisbury and Winchester — turning from it just after the view of Salisbury cathedral. In places it is difficult not to tread on pheasants so prolific are they, and you may see deer or a buzzard.

Walk 1	**4½ miles**	**Parts A B**
Walk 2	**6 miles**	**Parts A C**

A **TR** down the road and go over the crossroads. Beyond the school **TL** over a stile to follow a narrow path round the sports pitch and up into woods. Having passed behind a terrace of cottages, go over a stile next to a wooden gate ahead and, similarly, a second stile back into woods. This broad track eventually joins another from the left. Continue to a T-junction at the end. *(Look for the cathedral spire ahead).* Return to the previous junction and go straight on to pass a field to the right. At the end of this field **TR** and shortly **CL** back into the woods halfway along. **X** a metalled track and exit into a field ahead. Keeping the wire fence to the left, **X** the field, a broad gravel track, another field, and go up into woods through a very narrow gap in the hedgerow. Ahead is a T-junction.

B **TL** along and up to a crossing of paths. Slightly **FL** along a narrow path above a field. Descend into a leafy tunnel and **FR** past a house. Continuing just above, then merging with, the driveway, exit at the pub.

C **X** the stile into a field and **BR** to the far side to **X** another stile into the next field. **TR** around the edge of the field to a metal gate. Pass through and along a broad track, through another metal gate, and onto a road. **TR**, then **L** through a metal gate before a corrugated barn. **BL** across a field to a stile just beyond telephone wires. Over the stile **TR** to a wire gate below, and out onto a broad gravel track. **TL** into woods, past a broad tree break to the left, then **TL** up a narrower grass track. Exit over a stile onto a narrow path. Shortly **X** another stile to proceed along a stony track. **X** another stile between 2 gates to pass over the hill and down over 3 more stiles to a lane. **TL** to the pub.

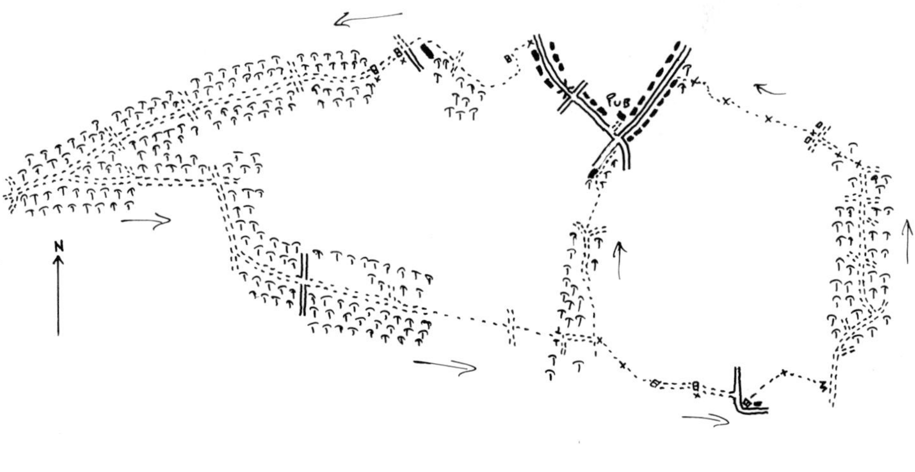

O.S. MAP NO. 172 : 693 679

From Keynsham turn left, and from Bath turn right, off the A4 at Saltford. Go through the residential area, then under the old railway bridge and along the riverbank to the pub. There is a large waterside car park.

HOURS:	Sunday	12.00 - 3.00	:	7.00 - 10.30
	Weekdays	11.00	———	11.00
	Saturday	11.00	———	11.00

This Courage house is run by Godfrey and Gillian Seagar. The pub sign depicts a Royal Marines landing-craft coxswain, so it is appropriate that Godfrey is an ex-Royal Marines Officer. The stone-walled bar and snug boast two original fireplaces with paintings above, one on wood shows river traffic in the early eighteenth century. An unusual feature is the large conservatory (known as 'the gazebo', though this seems to be a misnomer) overlooking the lock and weir and functioning as the dining-room. A reasonable range of standard recipes is offered and vegetarians should see the blackboard for the choice of the day. In addition to Courage Best and Directors, John Smith's Bitter is stocked.

There is no problem with children in 'the gazebo'.
Dogs are allowed on the premises.

Some varied forms of transport here: horses, boats, bikes, trains, (motor vehicles, if you feel pedantic) — and Shank's pony. While from Ogbourne St George you pass by coltish gallops, from Saltford Lock you climb to a fully-grown race course. This stands over 700 feet above the Avon from where you begin. See Bath down to the left, Bristol over to the right, Keynsham and Saltford out front. Descend through North Stoke, precariously perched (enough of this animal imagery!) on the hillside below, to recover with an easy stroll along the river and cycleway, which was once a railway line, back to the pub. The shorter walk plays safe with a casual circuit by the river and back along the cycleway.

Walk 1	**3½ miles**	**Parts A B D**
Walk 2	**6 miles**	**Parts A C D**

A **TL** back to the disused railway bridge. **TL** alongside it up to the cycleway and **X** the bridge over the river.

B Immediately **TL** again down a short steep slope to **X** a stile and continue along the bank, past the pub on the far bank, and over another stile. Pass through the hamlet of *Kelston Mills* to **X** another stile ahead and continue along the bank to a fence on to a main road. **TL** and carefully proceed through the village of *Swineford* to **TL** over a stile into the field opposite *The Swan* pub. *(Sorry, but there's no route other than the road).*

C Shortly **TL** on a stone bridge to twist down to its base and **X** a stile onto the broad track passing beneath it. **TL** along this track straight ahead through a sequence of 3 small metal gates by large ones with a stile intervening between the second and third. Exit onto a broad farm track, the farmyard to the left. Go through the metal gate opposite, **BR** to **X** a stile and follow a narrow path up to a main road. **TL**, then carefully **X** the road to go up a metalled track just before a cottage. Follow this up to the saddle between the two hills above. Approach a metal gate, but don't go through. **TL** up to **X** a stile by a wooden gate and on to the race course above.

Sharply **TL** along the rim, **X** a stile into a field and at the far end **CR** along the far edge away from the rim. Shortly **TL** through a gap in a stone wall and go along a broad grassy track to **X** a stile by a metal gate. Drop straight down to go through a metal gate onto a stony track. **TL** down through *North Stoke*, but **TR**, immediately before the lane curves left, along a track between 2 barns. Nearing the road, **X** a stile by a small wooden gate and go down the field to **X** a pair of stiles in a hedge gap below. Ahead is a final stile onto a broad gravel track. **TL** through a farm to carefully **X** the main road by *The Swan* and over a stile opposite.

D Follow the path along the river bank to a large bridge. Under a magnificent beech **X** a stile up to the cycleway and **TL**. Eventually, pass under a stone bridge, then shortly **TL** through a metal gate onto a lane. **TR** down to the riverside lane. **TL** to the pub.

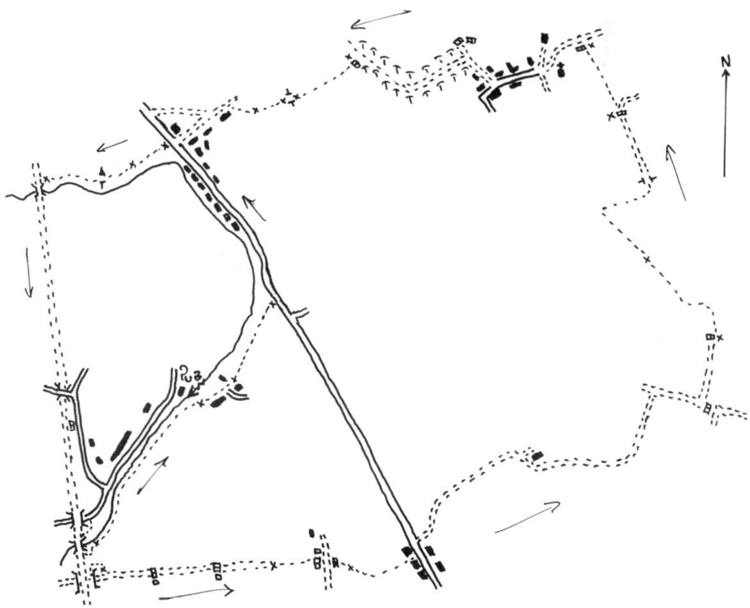

O.S. MAP NO. 174 : 235 633

From the south, turn right from the A346 just beyond Burbage at Stibb Green and, after about a half mile, the hotel is on the left just before the railway bridge.
From the north, turn left from the A346 just after crossing the Kennet and Avon canal at Burbage Wharf and the hotel is on the corner of the next junction.
There are two car parks either side of the road.

HOURS:	Sunday	12.00 - 3.00	:	7.00 - 10.00
	Weekdays	11.00 - 2.30	:	6.00 - 11.00
	Saturday	11.00 - 2.30	:	6.00 - 11.00

N.B. The restaurant is open only in the evening, except Sunday when it is open for lunch only. Daytime opening may be extended by request.

Built in 1863 by the Marquis of Ailesbury as a private hotel, it was intended for guests to Tottenham House — then the family residence on the nearby estate — arriving at the railway station that was then here. Today it has a lounge bar and buttery, decorated with pine panelling, chintz and a display of paintings by local artists, and an elegant restaurant.

A varied selection of bar snacks includes the intriguing prawn and sweetcorn oriental. In the restaurant more curiosity may be aroused, and satisfied, by a first course of tartelle of chicken coronation or coronets of smoked fish, followed by feuillette of game or medallions of beef cyrano or collop of venison black knight. Vegetarians and children are catered for. For ale drinkers there is Flowers' IPA, Mole's Cask Bitter, and a monthly-changing guest beer.

Children are welcome.
Dogs, however, must remain outside — unless resident.

Two walks through Savernake Forest and two more along the Kennet and Avon canal are all easy and straightforward. Together they offer some contrast between the effects of nature and of man upon the landscape: the enclosed forest with its constructed avenues and, alongside the mainline railway between London and Exeter, the more open canal with its wildlife (look out for kingfishers).

SAVERNAKE FOREST — THE SAVERNAKE FOREST HOTEL

Of interest is a triple-decker of crossings by the hotel: the road crosses the railway where the railway crosses the canal. It is here that the canal reaches its summit and a balanced supply of water eastwards and westwards is provided by the reservoir and pumping station at nearby Crofton, the destination for Walk 2. Similarly, Walk 3 follows the canal in the opposite direction, past Burbage Wharf to the picturesque setting of the lock at Wootton Rivers (page 95) and its friendly, knowledgeable keeper. Walks 1 and 4 pass through the forest, one of the most beautiful woodlands in southern England. You may see the King and Queen Oaks, and a column erected by the Marquis of Ailesbury in tribute to his uncle and his king from which extends an avenue towards the former family residence at Tottenham House. However, the forest remains private property and paths are closed for one day each year — in which case try the canal.

Walk 1	**3 miles**	**Parts A B D**
Walk 2	**3½ miles**	**Part E**
Walk 3	**5 miles**	**Part F**
Walk 4	**5½ miles**	**Parts A C D**

A **TL** along the road almost to the top of the hill. **TL** through a wooden gate along a broad grassy track on the edge of the hill. Soon after it passes along an avenue of beeches the path narrows to **CR** round to a gravel track just inside the forest. **TL** and go through a wooden gate. Immediately **CR** to a junction of tracks. Go ahead along a broad grass track.

B **TR** at the first intersection to the column.

C Go on to the third intersection. *(For a brief detour to the King and Queen Oaks* **TL** *and return).* Continue to the radial junction of *Eight Walks*. Sharply **TR** along the road to the second track on the **R**, just beyond open fields to left and right. **TR** up this broad metalled track, which soon becomes gravel, to **CL** parallel to the road. At a junction **TR** to a lane ahead. Again **TR** to the column, then **TL**.

D Go straight ahead along the broad avenue towards the distant *Tottenham House*. Pass through a metal gate onto a road and **TR** to the hotel.

E Go along the path opposite the hotel, down to the canal and on to *Crofton*. Return by the same route.

F Follow the path between the hotel and the railway, under the railway, down to the canal and on to *Wootton Rivers*. Return by the same route.

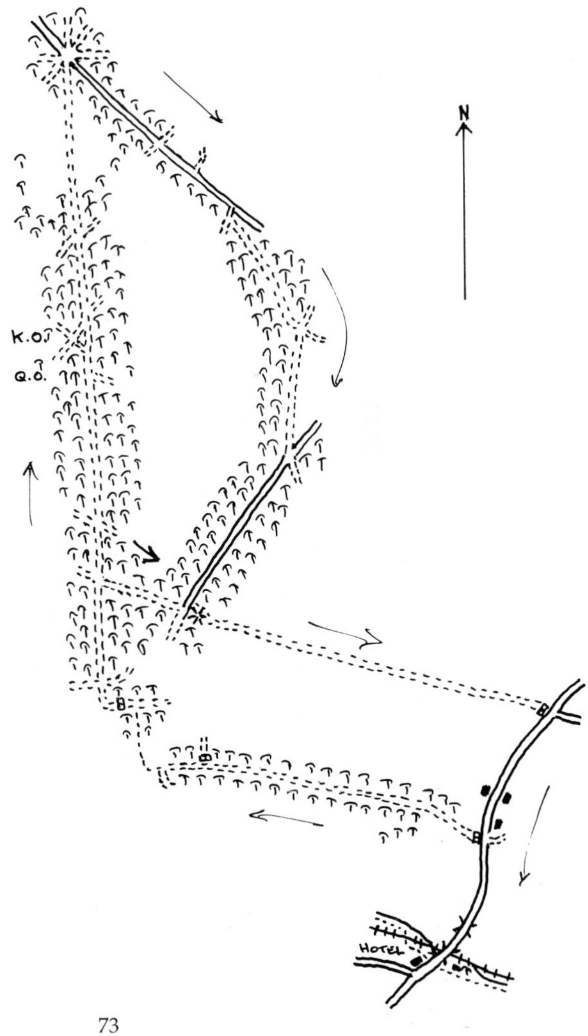

O.S. MAP NO. 173 : 932 614

From the A361, turn left about two and a half miles east of Semington roundabout.
Also from the A361, turn right about four and a half miles west of Devizes.
From the A365, turn right about two miles east of Melksham, and take the first right thereafter.
The inn lies alongside the canal.
Park in the inn car park

Situated on the side of the Kennet and Avon canal, this attractive stone-built Wadworth's house has an equally attractive and unusual decor employing a colourful and densely floral paper on walls and ceiling. There is an open fireplace with black-leaded grate below a mantleshelf and mirror. Chairs and tables are solid oak and well-used enough to add to the overall feeling of a homely Victorian cottage. A slightly surreal effect is achieved by the hand-painted milk churns employed as bar stools.

The bar, naturally, serves Wadworth's; Old Timer, 6X and IPA are stocked, while mulled wine is available in winter.

Adjacent to the bar is a dining area overlooking the canal. Snacks include jacket potatoes with stilton and ham, chilli or ratatouille filling. Alternatively, the main course offers goujons of salmon or a chicken pie (pastry-covered chicken in white wine and tarragon sauce with mushrooms). Vegetarians might try the cabbage, mushroom and nut bake. During summer there is a salad bar with local game pie. Finally, sail off with a longboat special — banana topped with toffee ice-cream and lashings of whipped cream covered with chocolate sauce and nuts.

A grass area with tables and seating is provided alongside the canal.

For those who prefer not to climb hills these three walks, like others in the collection, are of the 'flat and easy' variety. Partly along the Kennet and Avon canal and partly across adjacent pasture they are also short. Although, like any of the canal locations, it is possible to follow the towpath as far as you will. I was here in winter and what the photograph unfortunately cannot show is that those ducks had skated across the ice to reach their feed. Along Walk 2 a sign at a smallholding warns 'Trespassers will be eaten alive'.

Walk 1	**2½ miles**	**Parts A B**
Walk 2	**3 miles**	**Parts A C**
Walk 3	**4½ miles**	**Parts A D**

A **X** the canal and **TL** along the towpath. As the canal begins to **CL** and a far bridge appears, **TR** over a stile in the hedge. **BR** across the field, passing left of the right hand hedge, onto a dismantled railway track. **TR**, immediately go through a metal gate and again immediately **TL** over a stile into the far field. **BR** to a metal gate into the next field. Continue to a wooden gate onto a track, past houses, along to a road. Carefully **X** to a path opposite the filling station and continue between fields. Soon **CR** between houses to a road.

B **TR** along the road to a junction. Go through the wooden gate opposite into a field, **BR** to the **RH** corner to **X** a stile onto the dismantled railway track. **X** another stile into the field beyond. **BR** to **X** a stile in the centre of the **RH** hedge onto an embankment. **TL** to pass a farm and **X** a stile by a wooden gate to the bridge by the inn.

C **TR** along the lane and **TL** through a metal gate beyond the first house. Slightly **BR** to go through a metal gate in the hedge ahead. **BR** across a metalled drive to another metal gate in the far hedge. Slightly **BL** to **X** a stile in the far hedge onto a road. Carefully **X** the road and go along the drive opposite. **CR** to go through a white metal gate by the house. Ahead go through 3 gates by a smallholding and go on to **X** a stile onto the canal towpath. **TR** to the inn.

D **TL** along the lane which shortly becomes a track and curves right into a field. Here go on through a small wooden gate to a wooden fence. **TL** and immediately **R** over a bridge, then **R** again back onto the path. Continue ahead to go through a small metal gate and shortly **TR**, before the path turns left, through another metal gate into a field. Go straight ahead, past a farm and barn to the right, to **X** a wooden fence in the corner onto a broad grassy bridleway. **TR** to **X** a bridge and approach a farm. Go through a metal gate into the yard and immediately **TL** through another metal gate, then **TR** past the farm. Pass through another metal gate into the next field and on through yet another metal gate in the centre of the far hedge. Exit onto a road and carefully **X** over to pass through the wooden gate opposite. Go across the field to pass through the metal gate in the centre of the far hedge. Immediately **X** a stile into the field beyond. Ahead **TL** through a gap in the **LH** hedge, then **TR** to immediately **X** a stile by a metal gate. Ahead again **X** a stile by a metal gate onto the canal towpath. **TR** to the inn.

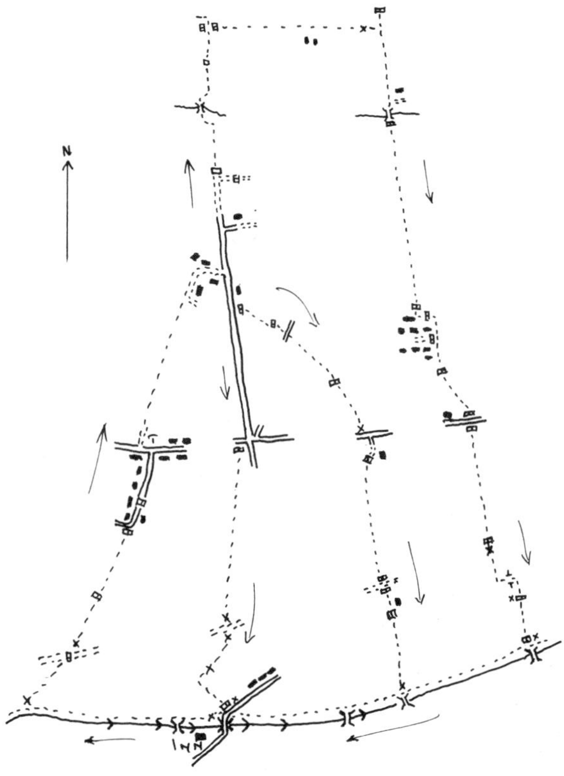

O.S. MAP NO. 184 (also 183) : 891 270

From the north, turn left from the A350 about two miles south of East Knoyle and two miles north of Shaftesbury. The pub is about a mile and a half on the left.
From the south, turn right from the A350 on the outskirts of Shaftesbury. The pub is about two miles on the left.
There is more than enough parking space outside the pub and round the village green.

HOURS:	Sunday	12.00 - 3.00	:	7.00 - 10.30
	Weekdays	11.00 - 2.30	:	6.00 - 11.00
	Saturday	11.00 - 2.30	:	6.00 - 11.00

The present building dates from around 1760 and, like so many country pubs, was built for estate employees. There is one split-level bar with a large open fireplace, by which is a seductively comfortable leather couch. Not being large, the bar is able to establish a cosy intimate atmosphere.

This Gibbs Mew house — Salisbury Best, Premium Bitter, and Graf Arco lager are available — is admirably run by Joe and Annie Duthie. Joe is a much-travelled man: born in Belfast, he moved to England as a boy, and has worked in Finland and the USA. He describes his politics as "slightly right of Gengis Khan". As the enormous home-made steak and kidney pie from the equally enormous bar menu was so delicious, I didn't argue the point. The fresh vegetables were crisp too — always a good sign.

The separate restaurant and its menu is similarly varied and, no doubt, just as good. Vegetarian dishes and children's meals may be had on request.

Both children and dogs may enter.

Pass through pasture and woodland from a village which appears briefly in Richard Condon's 'Prizzi' novels, though I saw no evidence of Mafia hoods. The nearest thing to a killer here is the short but very steep path from Cliff Cottage up the delightfully named Tittle Path Hill.

Walk 4 miles

TL and **X** the green to go along the road to *Donhead St Andrew.* Shortly **BR** along a hedge to **X** a stream and a stile into a field. Go up to **X** a pair of stiles in the far hedge. **X** this next field to a metal gate ahead. **BL** down, then up to the far corner. **X** the wire fence along the edge of the wood and go on to **X** another wire fence ahead. Go straight on through a gap in a wire fence, then **BR** up to and through a metal gate by a red-bricked house. Go through a wooden gate ahead and **TL**. Immediately **BR** up a grass path and again immediately **TR** through a gap in a hedge to go up to a road.

TR up to a T-junction and again **TR** to *Cliff Cottage.* Here **TL** through a narrow gap in the hedge flanking the cottage and driveway. Climb the steep path to a wire fence near the top. **TR**, keeping the fence to the left, and proceed along the edge of the wood to a road. *(To the left should be ancient earthworks).* **TL** along the road, past a lane to the left and another to the right. At the third junction **TR** steeply down a lane to a farm.

Immediately before a barn and a house, **TR** through a first metal gate, then immediately go through a second. Ignoring the gate almost opposite, **BL** to a third gate in the hedge ahead. Go through into the next field to **X** a pair of stiles over a stream at the far end. Go straight up the next field through a gap in a hedge, and on through a metal gate ahead. **TL** to pass through a metal gate onto a lane. Go through the metal gate opposite and **X** straight over to pass through a gap in a hedge. **X** the next field to go through a metal gate and immediately **TR** over a bridge. **BL** diagonally across the field to the **ULH** corner. **X** a stile, go on through a gap in a hedge and immediately **X** another stile into a wood. Go ahead along the edge of the wood beside a ditch and shortly pass to the left of an outbuilding. Exit onto a broken asphalt track and go along to a road. **TL** to the village.

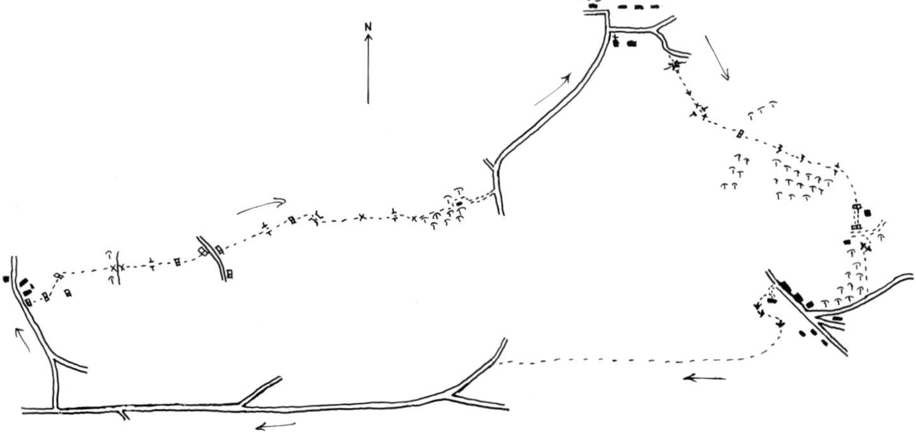

Avon valley (north) from Dundas aqueduct, Winsley

Avon Valley (south) from Dundas aqueduct, Winsley

O.S. MAP NO. 173 : 854 859

The inn is in the centre of the village on the B4040 between Badminton and Malmesbury. Parking on the premises is limited to six cars, though High Street and Church Street have space.

HOURS:	Sunday	12.00 - 2.30	:	7.00 - 10.30
	Weekdays	12.00 - 2.30	:	7.00 - 11.00
	Saturday	11.00	———	11.00

This Cotswold stone inn takes its unique name from the local Saxon hero, John Rattlebone, who was mortally wounded fighting for Edmund Ironside against Canute's Danes in 1017. He pressed a tile against the wound to prevent his bowels flowing out and continued fighting. The church owned the inn until the mid-nineteenth century.

There are two bars and a restaurant. The bars have stone walls and beamed ceilings. In the public bar there are traditional pub games: bar skittles, quoits, shove-halfpenny and shut-the-box. Hide away in the nooks and crannies of the lounge, decorated with memorabilia of the inn's history and a colourful collection of water jugs above the counter. Regular beers are Butcombe Bitter, and Wadworth's 6X, with several constantly changing guests. Bar snacks include daily 'specials'.

Mind your head as you enter the restaurant, though once inside there is a high gabled ceiling. Vegetarian meals are always available. Otherwise try local quails' eggs, pork with stilton and cream and a lemon syllabub to close. No separate children's meals, though.

David, Anne and Ian Rees are quite happy to play hosts to children and dogs.

SHERSTON — RATTLEBONE INN

Here I have tried to balance gently undulating fields and the Fosse Way (the Roman road between Bath and Cirencester) with a stretch of the upper Avon and the limestone village and country house of Easton Grey. However, on the shorter walks I have been unable to find a return route that avoids the road yet retains a manageable length.

Walk 1	**2½ miles**	**Parts A B**
Walk 2	**4½ miles**	**Parts A C D**
Walk 3	**6 miles**	**Parts A C E**

A From the inn **TR** and **R** again towards *Chippenham*. Halfway down the hill **TL** up concrete steps, pass across a cul-de-sac, along a tarmac path, and **X** a stile into a field. Go along a dry-stone wall to **X** another stile ahead and slightly **BR** to **X** another stile close to the middle of the far side. Pass between 2 stone out-buildings to a stone stile at the edge of a road. **TR** down the road, **X** a bridge, and **TL** up a lane to *Malmesbury*. About 400 yards along **TL** through a wooden gate along a stony track. Pass through a metal gate between 2 wooden pillars, and continue by a stone wall to arrive at a farm.

B **TL** down the lane and **L** again along the road to return to the inn.

C **TR** just before a stone barn into the farmyard. **TL** through a first metal gate and immediately **R** through a second, then through a small wooden gate between 2 single-storey stone out-buildings onto a path out of the yard. **BL** across a field, then **TR** above the river bank. Follow the line of the river across stiles and wooden fences *(see map)*, finally dropping down to a short stony track and out through a wooden gate onto a road. **TL** and **X** a bridge into the village of *Easton Grey*.

D Continue through the village and **TL** along the main road back to the inn *(about 2 miles)*.

E Over the bridge **TR** up a lane. At the top **X** over and go along a short gravel track, through a metal gate immediately ahead into a field. **BR** to the **URH** corner. Pass through a metal gate into the next field and **X** to a small wooden gate on the far side. Don't go through, but **TR** immediately before this gate through a broken wire gate. Slightly **BL** down to a metal gate. Go through and **TR** over the river. Continue through 2 gates — the first metal, the second wooden — along a broad grassy track. Go through a metal gate and **BR** up towards a line of trees ahead. *(You are now on the Fosse Way)*. **CR** to a metal gate. Go through and continue ahead. **X** a road onto a path, passing to the **L** of a house, and over a stream, then straight out onto and along another road. Shortly, go straight along the track ahead as the road curves away.

Continue along this track for about ½ mile where, soon after the hedgerow on the right includes a few trees, there is a metal gate in a gap in this hedge. **TR** into the field. Make for the farm and barn ahead, keeping the hedge to the right. **TR** through a wooden gate in this hedge into the next field. Keeping close to the hedge on the left, aim for a gap in the hedge ahead. Go through, **X** a broad grassy track, and pass immediately through a wooden gate into a field. Keeping close to the hedge on the right, make for the **URH** corner where, behind a small clump of trees, is a partially overgrown wooden gate. Ahead is *Sherston* church. Pass through into the next field. **TL** and, keeping close to the hedge, go round to a wooden gate in the middle of the **LH** side and out onto the road. **TR** and then **TL** through a wooden gate into a field. **BR** to the centre of the **RH** side and go through a gap in the hedge. **BL** to **X** a stone stile in the **ULH** corner. Go straight down the road, **TR** and go over the river into Sherston.

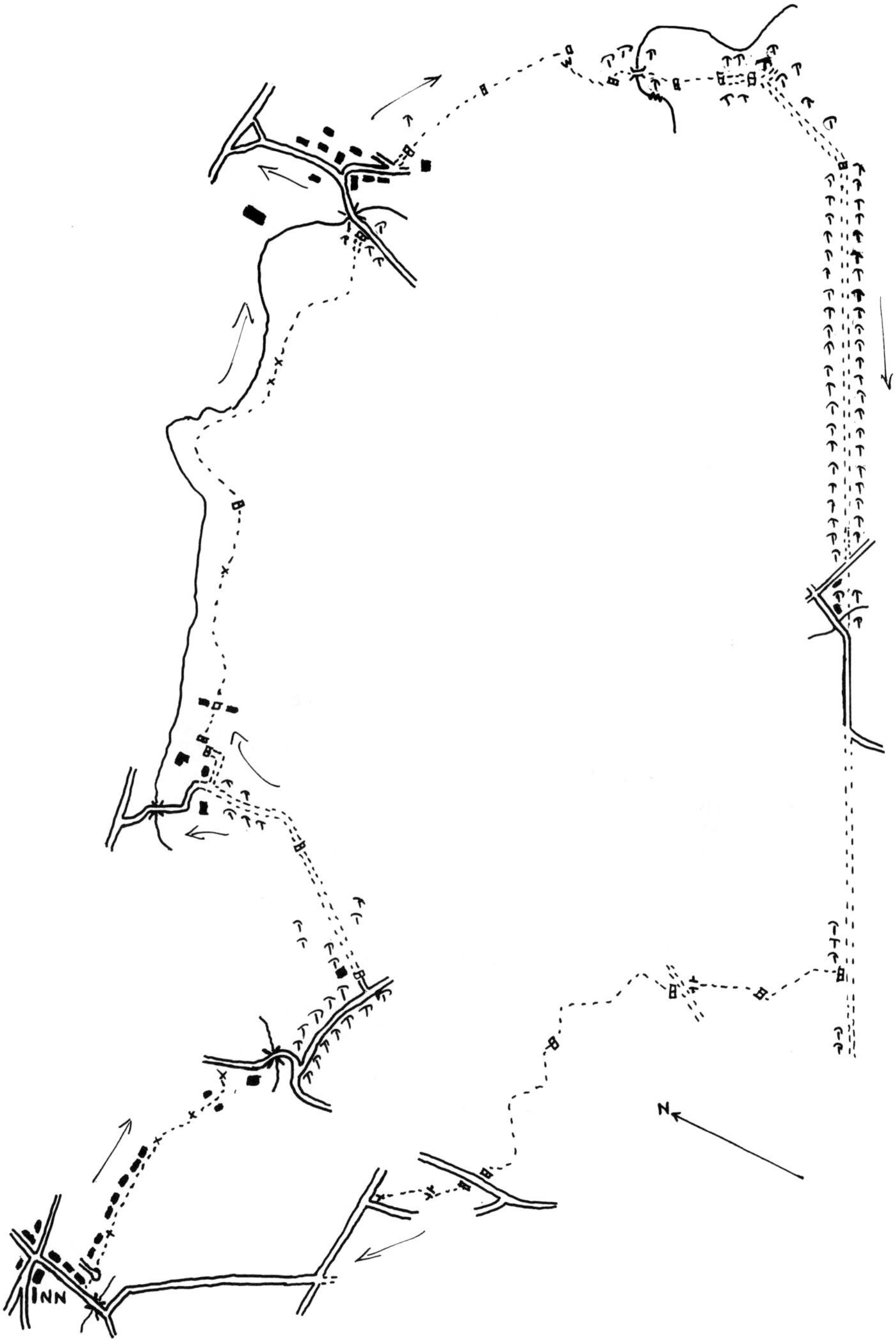
INN
N

O.S. MAP NO. 183 : 776 340

From the north, turn right from the B3092 Frome-Mere road two miles before Mere.
From the east, take the A303 and turn left through Mere on the B3092. Turn left again after two miles. The inn is on the left.
There is a car park just before the inn on the left. No other parking is available.

HOURS:	Sunday	12.00 - 3.00	:	7.00 - 10.30
	Weekdays	11.00 - 2.30	:	7.00 - 10.30
	Saturday	11.00 - 2.30	:	7.00 - 11.00

N.B. Friday evening is extended to 11.00.

A particularly dignified building with a Flemish bond brickwork front and two stone wings, it dates from the mid-eighteenth century. This is reflected in the lounge and dining-room with its large-mirrored dresser. There is an evening restaurant service, bar suppers and buffet lunches.

The restaurant menu always has a vegetarian dish. For those who continue to prefer meat and fish start with mushrooms and bacon in red wine with garlic mayonnaise, move to salmon with currants and stem ginger baked in pastry with a chervil and tarragon cream sauce, and cleanse the palate with a baby coconut 'pina colada'. While children's meals are not normally available, they can be arranged.

Unfortunately, the only real ales stocked are Bass and Charrington IPA.

Children are welcome. Dogs too.

Dorset's Stour rises here before flowing into the Channel at Christchurch. In some respects, however, this location has an architectural interest. The walks pass through Stourhead House estate; by the house and lakes, past an obelisk and St Peter's Pump, moved from Bristol and placed over the source of the Stour which flows underground to emerge in the lakes below. Visit Alfred's Tower, said to be built on the site where the king declared resistance against the Danes. By the road near the inn is the splendidly ornate, early fifteenth century Bristol High Cross, commemorating monarchs who benefitted the city; it was moved here in 1765. Beyond, across the lake, is the neo-classical Pantheon built in 1753. All walks have steep, yet short, ascents and descents. Walk 1 is the shortest but has the steepest paths.

STOURTON — THE SPREAD EAGLE INN

Walk 1	**2 miles**	**Parts A B E G**
Walk 2	**4½ miles**	**Parts A C D E G**
Walk 3	**5½ miles**	**Parts A C F G**

A **TR** up the road to *Stourhead House* gateway. **TL** along the drive, past the front of the house, and go through a metal gate. **TL** through 2 wooden gates to a lodge ahead. **TL** over a stile, left of a metal gate before the lodge. **TR** to the end of the metal fence, then **BL** steeply down into the wood to a broad track below. **TR** to pass through a wooden gate into a field.

B **BL** between 2 lakes and up a very steep path to a broad grassy track above. **TL** and immediately **TR** along a track to another broad grassy track. Again **TL** and immediately **TR** to **X** 2 more tracks ahead, then steeply down a narrow path to a stile below. **X** onto a broad track and **TL** to a stile by a wooden gate.

C Follow the path gently uphill to *St Peter's Pump* and **X** to the far side. Continue ahead, then **BL** up to the **ULH** corner to **X** a stile in a wire fence. **TL** on a path by a road to *Alfred's Tower*. **TL** along a track into a wood. About ½ mile on **TR** at a crossing of paths and shortly arrive at another similar crossing.

D **TL** to go along above a field, then soon emerge from the wood and go through a series of gates. Shortly merge with another track from the left to approach a stile by a wooden gate.

E **X** the stile and continue along past a new stone cottage and round to a wooden gate by a lake.

F Go on down to **BR** along a metalled track onto a lane. Go on to **FL** to the hamlet of *Gasper* about 1 mile ahead. Immediately after the second building on the left, **TL** through trees by the drive to **X** a stile into a field. Descend to the **LRH** corner and **BR** through a line of trees to a small wooden gate in the **LLH** corner of the adjacent field. Go through into a spinney to **X** a bridge. As the stream curves left, go straight on to **X** another bridge, on through a small wooden gate and **X** a stile into a field. Go up to a metal gate and out onto a lane by a bend. **TR** past cottages to the next bend and **TL** through a wooden gate. Go straight on between a copse above and a lake below, then **BR** down to a wooden gate by the lake.

G Go through to a road and **TL** to the inn.

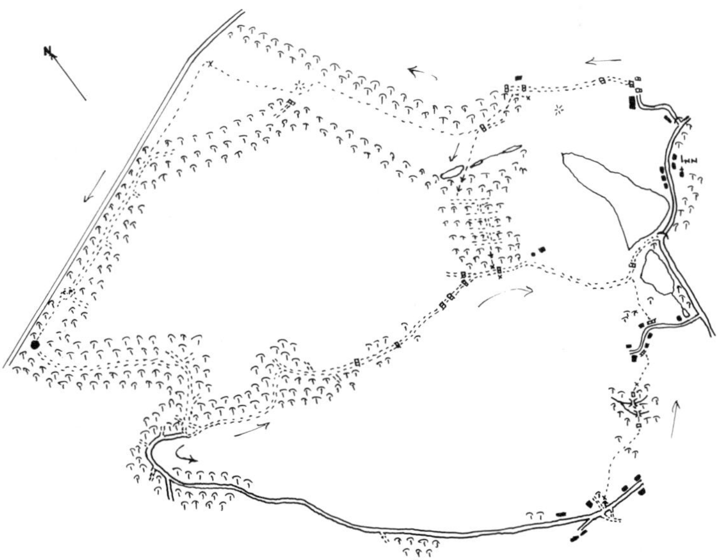

O.S. MAP NO. 183 : 872 314

Take the A350 to East Knoyle and turn right (coming from the north) or left (from the south) to the top of the hill.
There is no car park, so use the roadside and the edge of the green opposite.

HOURS:	Sunday	12.00 - 3.00	:	7.00 - 10.30
	Weekdays	11.00 - 2.30	:	6.00 - 11.00
	Saturday	11.00 - variable	:	6.00 - 11.00

Andrew and Doreen Knight run this freehouse overlooking the Vale of Blackmoor — in fine weather sit outside on the green and enjoy the view. Andrew has farmed in Berkshire and Cornwall and, not surprisingly, is interested in country pursuits. The pub, of brick and stone with thatched roof, was originally three cottages built in the mid-seventeenth century.

The public bar has darts and pool, while the comfortable split-level L-shaped lounge has an inglenook fireplace. There is a skittle alley cum children's room, though no children's meals are available on the menu. For adults there are bar snacks and home-made specials, including vegetarian, listed on a blackboard.

Andrew regularly keeps six real ales, though the selection may vary. I saw Usher's Best, Wadworth's 6X, Marston's Pedigree, King and Barnes' Sussex Bitter, Ringwood Best, and Bateman's XXXB — Burrow Hill Farmhouse Cider too.

Children in the children's room, naturally.
Dogs in the public bar.

Woodland, pasture, a beautiful village church and a fine hilltop view, west to Stourton and Stourhead (page 83) and south to Duncliffe Hill by Shaftesbury, are to be enjoyed on these walks. Although both are of similar length, the shorter is also the easier.

THE GREEN — THE FOX AND HOUNDS

Walk 1	**3 miles**	**Parts A B**
Walk 2	**4 miles**	**Parts A C**

A **TL** from the pub and immediately **L** up the lane. **TL** up the path to *Bay Tree House*. Shortly **TR** through a gap in a line of firs and immediately over a stile into a field. **TR** along the edge of the field and back garden fences. Follow the edge and **TL** uphill to a metal gate in the **URH** corner. Exit onto a lane, **X** over, and up to the track to *Haddon Hill.* Shortly the track divides in 4 directions. Take the extreme **L** path. **FR** of a sign for riders to *Keep to Main Track*, ignoring the yellow arrow indicating a path to the left. After some 400 yards sharply **TR** downhill to a narrow lane. **TL** and pass some farm buildings on the left. At a junction with another lane **TR** towards *Mere.* After about 100 yards, passing on the left a large cottage sited 45° to the lane, **TL** up a bridlepath, keeping farm buildings to the left. Pass through 2 wooden gates into a field. **BL** across the field to the **ULH** corner. Pass through a small wooden gate, along a narrow grassy ridge and down through a farmyard to the church. Follow the road past the church. Continue past the junction to *Charnage* into the village. Pass round an S-bend to a stone bungalow, *Frickers Mead*, opposite a white-bricked house, *Willows*.

B Just beyond **TL** up a gravel track, **X** a short causeway and go through a metal gate. **BL** across to the **ULH** corner and **X** a low wooden fence. **X** a stile ahead into the corner of a wood and immediately go through a small wooden gate and wire gate into the next field. **X** to the **ULH** corner and pass through a metal gate onto a metalled track. **TL** and follow the track round to the road. **TR** to the pub.

C Continue along the road and **TL** opposite *Broadmead Farm* along the drive to *Arathoon*. Shortly **CL** and **CR** past a farmhouse and continue on a gravel track through a large wooden gate. By a cottage the track becomes a narrow path. Continue over a bridge and through another wooden gate. Immediately **TL** over a wooden fence to continue above a stream and tree line, and shortly **BR** up to pass through a wire gate onto a broad grassy track. **TL** to a metal gate ahead. Go through and **TR** across the field. In the middle of the hedge is a metal gate. Go through and **X** directly over the next field to a small wooden gate in the middle of a wire fence on the far side. Immediately **X** a wooden bridge over a stream and pass through a second small wooden gate. **X** the field ahead, keeping close to the hedge on the left. Pass through a break in the trees on the far side into the next field. **BR** towards an old oak near the **URH** corner. Beyond, pass through a wooden gate onto a broad grassy track. **TL** and, about 40 yards along, **TR** over a wooden fence. **X** the field, keeping the hedge to the left, and **CR** down to the lowest corner. **TL** through a small gap in the hedge and wire fence into woods. Shortly **X** a stream, go over a wire fence and climb the path, keeping the fence to the left. At the top exit into an open grassy area. **BL** to a small wooden gate back into the woods. Go through, following the path until it too emerges through a small wooden gate into another open area. **BR** to the **ULH** corner. Go through a wooden gate onto a track leading back to the pub.

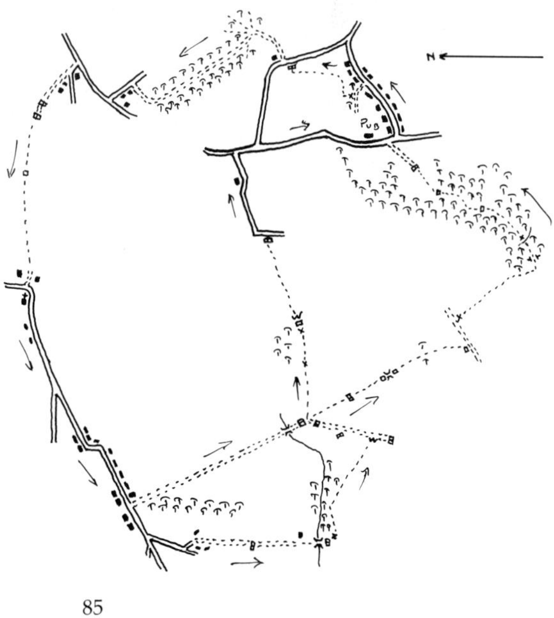

TOLLARD ROYAL — THE KING JOHN HOTEL

O.S. MAP NO. 184 : 944 178

From the north, take the A350 to Shaftesbury and then the B3081 towards Ringwood.
From the east, take the A354 towards Blandford and turn right on the B3081 through Sixpenny Handley.
Parking space is allocated for twenty six cars, overspill to the pond one hundred yards down the road.

HOURS:	Sunday	12.00 - 3.00	:	7.00 - 10.30
	Weekdays	11.00 - 2.30	:	6.00 - 11.00
	Saturday	11.00 - 3.00	:	6.00 - 11.00

N.B. Restaurant evenings only, except Sunday and Monday.

This dignified mid-nineteenth century building of brick and flint has a comfortable L-shaped bar and separate restaurant. Bar snacks are readily available (except Monday evening). In the restaurant Mr Symes serves starters of stilton stuffed mushrooms and lobster bisque. Vegetarians may choose a main course from vegetable pasta or vegetable stir-fry. Fish fanciers might like to try the darn of salmon or scallops patissier. Children are catered for. Real ale drinkers may choose from Fuller's London Pride or Oakhill Yeoman Ale.

Children may come into the restaurant.
No dogs inside, please.

Two walks that pass over Win Green, which at 909 feet above sea level is the highest point on Cranborne Chase, give perhaps the best view in this collection. Look south-east across Dorset to The New Forest (Nomansland, page 63) and Hampshire beyond — just below the horizon is Horton Tower, an eighteenth century folly; south towards the hills above Blandford; south-west across Blackmoor Vale to the Dorset Gap; west to the sharp hills above Sherborne; north-west to Shaftesbury and, just to the right, Semley Hill (Semley, page 77); north to the plantation around Old Wardour Castle (Ansty, page 13) and, on the horizon, the edge of Salisbury Plain; east along the Ebble Valley and the downs above Ebbesbourne Wake (page 42).

Walk 1	**5 miles**	**Part A**
Walk 2	**6 miles**	**Parts A B**

A Walk down the road to the village centre. At the pond **TL** up the lane. **FL** at some farm buildings. **X** the stile next to a metal gate. **CL** up the path. Go through a metal gate and drop down to a stile and metal gate below. **X** the stile, and follow the line of trees to the left up to a metal gate above. **X** the stile by the gate and continue uphill. At the top **TR** and **X** the stile ahead. Go on towards a small clump of trees and triangulation point. *(This is Win Green).* Go on down to the stony track from the left. *(This is an old drovers' track).* Follow it to a junction of tracks and a sign *By-way to Tollard Royal.* For Walk 1 take this route back to the village.

B **FL** of this latter track and, just beyond, **TR** along the road. At a T-junction **TR** along a broad stony track and through 2 metal gates. In the middle distance across the field ahead is a line of trees; aim for the extreme **RH** end. *(If the field is sown, keep to the **RH** edge just below the ridge of the hill, turning **L** at the end).* Just before this line of trees, exit over a stile by a metal gate onto a broad grassy track. **X** the stile next to another gate opposite and, keeping close to the **LH** edge, go to the far end of the next field. Here go over a stile by a metal gate and down a broad grassy path across the next field to a metal gate at the bottom. Continue along the now level grass path for about 50 yards, then **BR** up the steep slope to a small metal gate in the wire fence above. Go through and along a broad grass strip between 2 fields, through a double metal gate at the end of a line of beeches and, keeping close to the wire fence on the right, drop down over the hill to a small metal gate. Go through and down to a second small metal gate into the village.

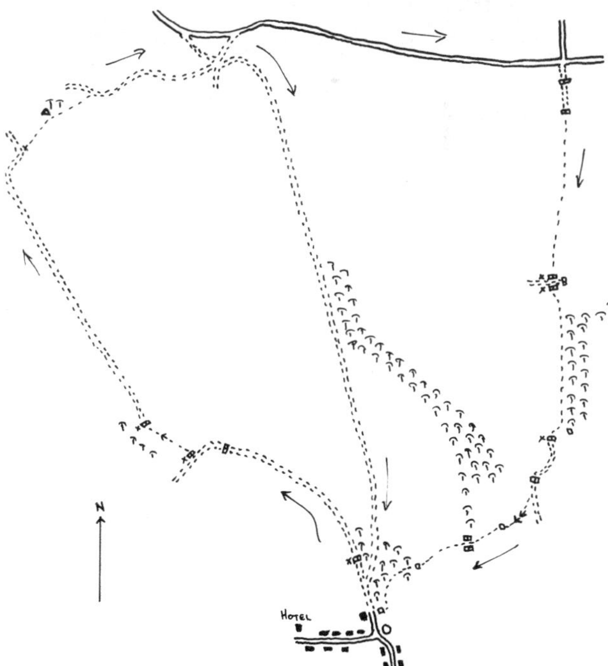

O.S. MAP NO. 184 : 124 373

From Salisbury, take the minor road off the A345 through Old Sarum and turn left over the Avon. The Bridge is about two miles up the valley.
From Amesbury, take the minor road down the Avon valley to 'The Woodfords'. The Bridge is about three miles on.
From the A360, cross the A303 near Stonehenge and continue south to take the first left to a T-junction at Middle Woodford. Turn left again and The Bridge is about a mile further on.
There is ample parking opposite the pub in the car park by the river, and either side of the pub.

HOURS:				
	Sunday	12.00 - 3.00	:	7.00 - 10.30
	Weekdays	10.30 - 2.30	:	6.00 - 11.00
	Saturday	10.30 - 2.30	:	6.00 - 11.00

N.B. Summer hours are extended.

The Bridge is a painted stone and slate-roofed building reputed to be of seventeenth century origin. It has a bar, pool room and a restaurant, and has recently been refurbished. A Gibbs Mew house, the bar serves Wiltshire Bitter and Salisbury Best, Graf Arco lager and Copperhead draught cider. A plethora of bar snacks extends beyond fifty items and the restaurant menu should have something to satisfy most tastes, including vegetarians and children. The Berrys are both ex-naval personnel with fifteen years in the licensed trade.

Children are welcome to dine with their parents.
Dogs stay outside.

The Woodfords are distributed along Wiltshire's other Avon before it flows through Salisbury to the sea at Christchurch. A pretty location, and one of the few in the Wiltshire part of the valley from which it is possible to walk any distance without bumping into some military establishment. The route passes along the river in two places and offers an optional extension to Stonehenge, an extra 2½ miles in all.

Walk 6 miles (8½ miles to Stonehenge)

TL along the road to *Boreland House* on the left. **TR** along a gravel track opposite. Follow it round to briefly join another track ahead, continuing straight on as the latter swings left. Eventually, sharply **TR** to **X** a bridge over the river and almost immediately another bridge over a millrace. Pass the millhouse and continue along the drive to *Great Durnford*. **TL** along the road, past *Manor House School* and, immediately beyond *Greystone House* ,**FL** up a gravel track. Drop down to pass through a metal gate, then **FR** to go through a second metal gate. Keeping close to a hedge on the right, go ahead to **X** a stile. Continue ahead to **TR** through a small metal gate just before the end of the field. **FL** down to a very narrow path through the spinney edging the river. **TL** over a bridge across a cutting and on over another bridge across the river, then **BR** over a brick bridge across another cutting. Pass by a red-bricked house, then **CL** to **X** a stile by a metal gate onto the driveway and **TR** to a road.

TL along the road for about 500 yards, then **TR** up a lane to *Springbottom Farm*. Go over the hill and down to the farm. *(To Stonehenge: **FR** beyond the farm along a track up to the monument about 1¼ miles distant. Return to this point).* Between the house and barns beyond sharply **TL**, then **CR** along a broad gallop beside a paddock fence. About 1 mile ahead this broad track curves left and straightens again before passing a T-junction with a track from the left. Here **TR** through a gap in a hedge and climb up into the wood above. **BL** up to **X** a stile by a metal gate and continue along the edge of the wood to **X** another stile by a metal gate onto a road. Carefully **X** the road and **BR** down the track next to the cottage opposite. The track shortly narrows to a path which crosses a driveway to continue down to the river and the first bridge at the beginning. **FR** to retrace steps to the pub.

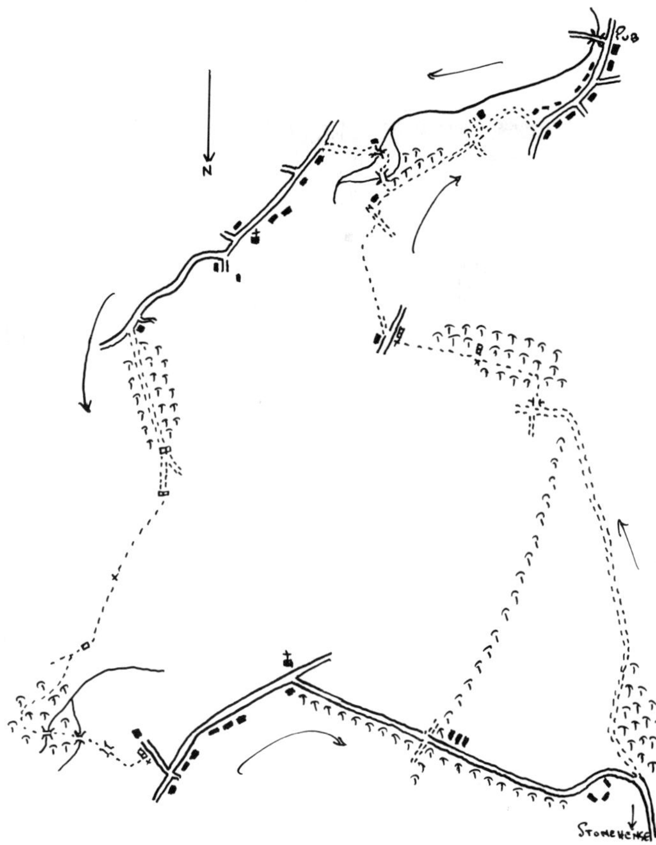

O.S. MAP NO. 184 : 245 236

On the A27 about one mile east of the junction with the A36.
Park on the road or, preferably, the car park at the rear.

HOURS:	Sunday	12.00 - 3.00	:	7.00 - 10.30
	Weekdays	11.00 - 3.00	:	7.00 - 11.00
	Saturday	11.00	———	11.00

A friendly village pub of painted brick and slate with a plaster and beamed interior. A bricked open fireplace with a log fire supplies winter warmth. There is one bar and a separate games room with a round pool table. Owned by Wiltshire Brewery, Old Grumble, Old Devil, and the new Stonehenge Real Ginger Beer (brewed from fresh root ginger) are available, together with Stowford Press draught cider.

The daily-changing menu on the blackboard offers traditional English home-cooked food like hotpot, liver and onions, and fisherman's pie.

En suite accommodation is available.

Children are welcome.
Dogs too.

A very economic walk, an apparently easy approach steadily gains height to Pepperbox Hill and Dean Hill, a long ridge with an impressive drop down to the other side, to provide a dominating view northwards to the Clarendon Way (Pitton, page 69) and north-west across Salisbury. Make a short detour to see The Pepperbox, the folly which gives the hill its name.

Walk 1	**5½ miles**	**Parts A B**
Walk 2	**6 miles**	**Parts A C**
Walk 3	**7 miles**	**Parts A D**

A **TR** along the road to the junction to *Downton* on the left. Here **TR** along a narrow path between 2 cottages to **X** a stile into a field. Ahead **X** another stile in the centre of the **RH** fence into the adjacent field. **BL** to **X** another stile in the far **RH** corner. Keeping close to the wire fence on the left, go on to **CR** around farm buildings ahead. **X** a junction of tracks to briefly go along a broad level track, then almost immediately **TL** past a couple of trees to **CR** along the edge of a copse. Drop down to merge with a broad track from the left and continue ahead, climbing steadily. *(Notice a human grave where the track becomes a path).* Eventually, above on Pepperbox Hill, **X** a stile by a metal gate onto the ridge path. *(Remember this location).* **TL** to The Pepperbox. Return and continue along the ridge path.

B About 1½ miles from The Pepperbox and about 100 yards past the second junction to the left, **TR** through a gap in the wire fence along a bridleway. Drop down to **TR** towards a copse. **TL** up a path within the edge of this copse. Continue on this path to **CR** and gently descend into a bridleway, past a farm to the road. **TL** for the inn.

C Eventually merge onto a lane from a farm to the right. About ½ mile ahead **TR** opposite a paddock along a track past a radio mast. Follow this track past a farm to a road below. **TR** to *Whiteparish* and again **TR** to the inn.

D Eventually merge onto a lane from a farm to the right. About ¾ mile ahead **TR** down a road and pass a radio mast. Just before a fork in the road **TL** over a stile in a hedge. Make way to the **ULH** corner, so **TL** along the same hedge and **TR** at the end of the field up to a stile into a wood. Do not enter, but again **TR** along the edge of the same field and the wood. At the far end exit over a stile onto a track and immediately **X** another stile into the next field. Keeping close to the left hand wire fence, **TR** at the far end and shortly **X** a stile onto a road. **TL** and shortly **TR** along a grassy bridleway to, eventually, exit onto a road. Go along the grassy track opposite, through a large white wooden gate, and directly across a field to exit over a stile onto a metalled track to *Blaxwell Farm*. **TL** and immediately go through a metal gate, then **TR** through another metal gate to pass behind barns. **X** a stile into a field and pass through the metal gate opposite into the next field. In the centre of the **LH** hedge **TL** through a metal gate into the adjacent field. **TR** along the same hedge to exit through a large white wooden gate onto a gravel drive between bungalows. Ahead is a road. **TR** for the church and the inn.

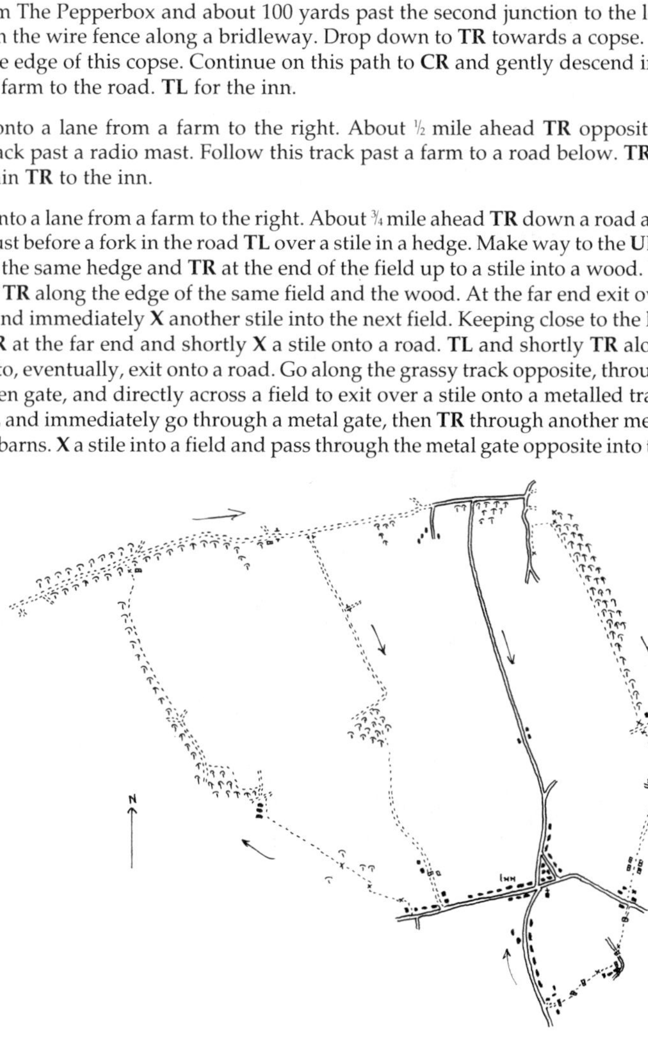

O.S. MAP NO. 172 (also 173) : 799 609

From Bath, take the A36 and turn left on the B3108 towards Bradford-on-Avon. From Bradford-on-Avon, take the B3108.
Approximately thirty cars may park in the pub car park, and a village car park is now under construction.

HOURS:	Sunday	12.00 - 2.30	:	7.00 - 10.30
	Weekdays	11.45 - 2.30	:	6.00 - 11.00
	Saturday	11.45 - 2.30	:	6.00 - 11.00

At the Seven Stars both exterior and interior are of Bath stone. This is complemented with dark stained pine and two open fireplaces with crackling logs in winter. At the short end of the L-shaped bar a raised area with settee and upholstered armchair creates a cosy sitting-room effect. Enquire whether you may play the piano just inside the entrance. Tony and Carol Coates keep Usher's Best, Ruddle's Best, and County. A range of home-made bar snacks and 'specials' is available, including vegetarian, though no children's meals.

No children or dogs inside.

The second of two locations in the lovely Avon valley by Bath explores the north and east banks as the river swings north at Limpley Stoke. The routes together pass along the towpath of the Kennet and Avon canal and over Dundas aqueduct which carries it over the river and the railway, along the steeply wooded bank to cross farmland above.

WINSLEY — THE SEVEN STARS

Walk 1	**4 miles**	**Parts A B D**
Walk 2	**6½ miles**	**Parts A C D**

A **TL** and enter a lane as the road turns right. **TL** and **TR** with the lane, then immediately **TR** again over a stone stile set in the wall. Follow the path over a second stile to **FL** ahead at a short brick and stone wall. This narrow path drops steeply down, sometimes in steps, past houses and across a field to a canal bridge. **X** the bridge and **TR** along the towpath to eventually **X** *Dundas* aqueduct. Continue over a small lifting bridge round to a larger humped bridge to the far towpath and **TR** back over the aqueduct.

B Go directly up the path ahead, over 2 stiles into the wood above. **TR** along a wire fence to exit onto a lane. Again **TR** along the lane for about ½ mile to where it makes a sharp right hand curve round *Conkwell Grange*. Here **TL** over a stile in the stone wall and X the field to pass through a metal gate to the right of a copse ahead. Follow the stone wall round to go through another metal gate ahead. Aiming for the houses ahead, make way to a stile in the far stone wall, onto another lane and **TR** to a T-junction.

C **TL** down steps into the field below and follow the river bank path, beyond the woods to **BR**, opposite a tunnel under the railway, up to a stile. **X** the stile, go on through a metal gate, then a wooden gate into a farmyard. **TL** onto a lane. **TL** along the lane to a cottage below on the left, opposite which is a stile in the hedge. **TR** over the stile and climb up to **X** another stile on the edge of the treeline above. Climb up through the wood to **TL** then sharply **R** around a blockage across the path. Pass through a gap in a stone wall, then **TL** to go under an arch and **CR** around to a road. **X** the road and **BL** along a lane opposite. At the green ahead **FR** to pass through a small wooden gate next to the last cottage into a field. **BR** to a small wooden gate in the right hand hedge and exit onto a main road.

Carefully **X** the road and **TL** along the pavement opposite to shortly **TR** up the drive to *Inwoods*. **FL** into a farmyard and **BL** to pass through a metal gate. **TR** along a stone wall to pass through another metal gate into a wood. Go straight on and through a third metal gate to pass along the outside edge of the wood and through a fourth metal gate ahead. Immediately go through a broken metal gate and **TL** through a gap in a wire fence. **BR** to go through yet another metal gate, then **TR** along the edge of another wood. Ahead **X** a broad track and stile to meander along the edge of the same wood to **X** a stone stile out onto a lane. **TL** and go round past a farmhouse to **TR** into a field immediately beyond. Keeping close to the right hand hedge, **TR** through a gap into the adjacent field and **TL** along the same hedge to pass through a metal gate onto another lane. **TL** along the lane and **FR** to a T-junction about a mile ahead.

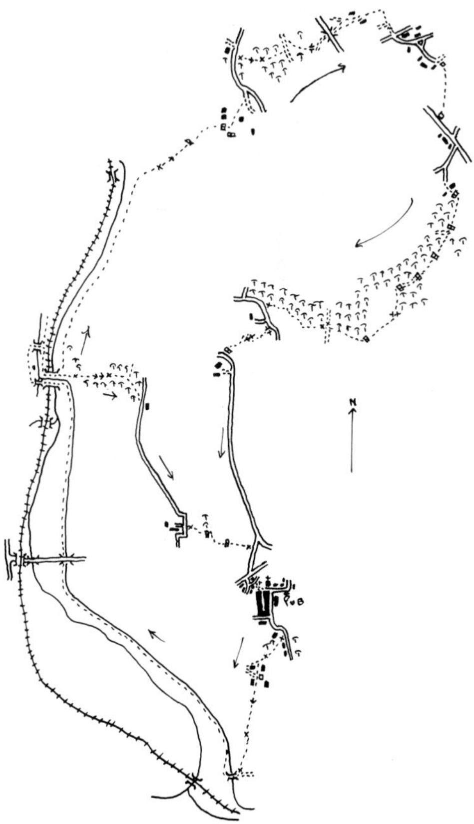

D **X** into *Late Broads* opposite. Shortly **TL** into *Millburn Close* and immediately **TR** along a footpath between new houses. **FL** past the church onto the main road and **TR** for the pub.

O.S. MAP NO. 173 : 197 633

From Marlborough, take the A345 south, turn left at Clench Common and take the next two left turns to the pub.
From Pewsey, take the B3087 east for about half a mile, turn left over the railway and canal, then first right to the pub.
Park in the pub car park, the main village street or the village hall car park.

HOURS:	Sunday	12.00 - 3.00	:	7.00 - 10.30
	Weekdays	11.00 - 3.30	:	6.30 - 11.00
	Saturday	11.00 - 3.30	:	6.30 - 11.00

This sixteenth century thatched pub is run by John and Rosa Jones. In the mid-sixties, John worked for the Playboy Club and Penthouse Club in London, later for Ladbroke's Casino — plenty of anecdotes there, I'm sure. With walls of old warm-toned bricks, wattle and daub and a wealth of beams, there are two bars and a restaurant. Bar snacks include deep fried clams and there is an ample restaurant menu which includes vegetarian and children's meals. John regularly stocks Wadworth's 6X and, in addition, there is one guest ale.

Bed and breakfast is available if you want to make a weekend of it.

Children and dogs are welcome, but only the dogs have to be on a lead.

Another pleasant walk over farmland and the 950 feet Martinsell Hill at the eastern end of the Tan Hill Walk and the Vale of Pewsey. There are two short steepish sections on the way up and a very steep section down — it's easier that way. Some fine views west along the valley's northern hills, east along the Kennet valley towards Newbury, and south-west towards Chute (page 59).

Walk 1	**4½ miles**	**Parts A B D**
Walk 2	**5½ miles**	**Parts A C D**

A **TR** along the road and **FL** by a house called *Martinsell* along a track to **X** a stile by a metal gate.

B Immediately **TL** through a gap in a wire fence beside another metal gate. Keeping close to the wire fence on the left, go to the far end to **TL** through a metal gate. **TR** to **X** a stile by a metal gate, and **BR** across a field to go through a metal gate onto a lane. **TR** and follow the lane round to join a road. **TR** again and follow this lane up the hill to **TL** over a stile between 2 gates.

C Follow the track uphill and through a gap in a wire fence into a field. **TR** down to the corner to pass through a gap in the hedge and onto a broad track. **TL** up to a T-junction and **TL** again along to a road. **X** over and **X** a stile between 2 gates.

D Follow a broad grass path to and across the summit. Go through a small wooden gate and along to **X** a stile. **BL** steeply down to a track in a narrow gorge. Immediately, go through a metal gate and follow the track down to and along a lane. TL through a small wooden gate just past a group of cottages and, keeping close to the left hand wire fence, follow the path through a wire gate, onto a track, through a metal gate, behind some cottages and through another metal gate into a farmyard. **TL** up a track out of the yard and **TR** through a metal gate into a field. Keeping close to the wire fence on the right, make way to a wire gate in the centre of the far side and left of the copse ahead. Go through to another field and **BL** at the end of the copse down and across to a metal gate behind the shed to the right of the house ahead. Go through, **TR** up the drive and **L** along a road. **TR** at a T-junction ahead and go on down to the pub.

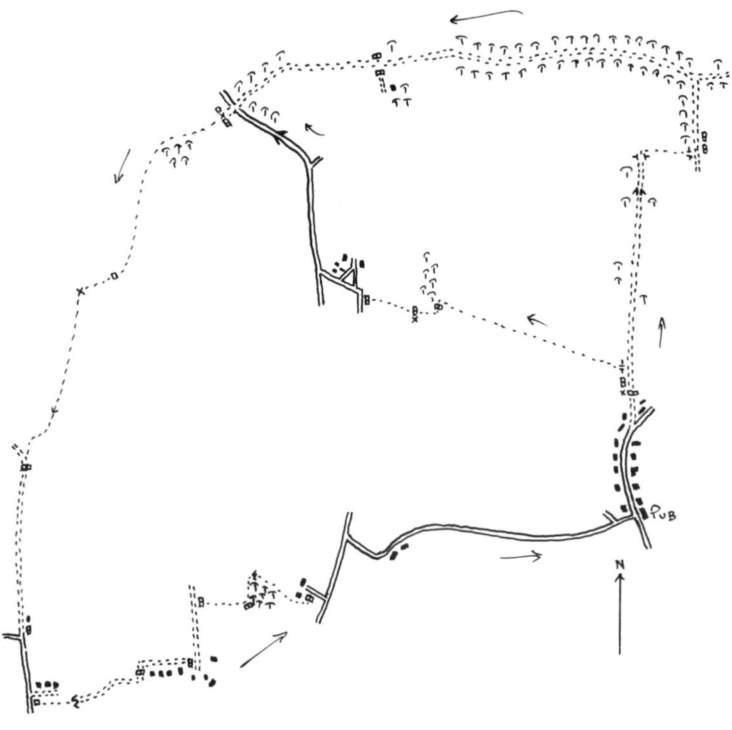

Cold Ashton from Beek's Farm, Pennsylvania

Blackmoor Vale from The Green